The Novel,

Who Needs It?

~

Also by Joseph Epstein

Gallimaufry: A Collection of Essays, Reviews, Bits (2020)

Charm: The Elusive Enchantment (2018)

The Ideal of Culture: Essays (2018)

Where Were We?: The Conversation Continues, with Frederic
  Raphael (2017)

Wind Sprints: Shorter Essays (2016)

Frozen in Time (2016)

Masters of the Games: Essays and Stories on Sport (2015)

A Literary Education and Other Essays (2014)

Distant Intimacy: A Friendship in the Age of the Internet, with Frederic
Raphael (2013)

Essays in Biography (2012)

Gossip: The Untrivial Pursuit (2011)

The Love Song of A. Jerome Minkoff: And Other Stories (2010)

Fred Astaire (2008)

In a Cardboard Belt!: Essays Personal, Literary, and Savage (2007)

Friendship: An Exposé (2006)

Alexis de Tocqueville: Democracy's Guide (2006)

Fabulous Small Jews (2003)

Envy (2003)

Snobbery: The American Version (2002)

Narcissus Leaves the Pool: Familiar Essays (1999)

Life Sentences: Literary Essays (1997)

With My Trousers Rolled: Familiar Essays (1995)

Pertinent Players: Essays on the Literary Life (1993)

A Line Out for a Walk: Familiar Essays (1991)

The Goldin Boys: Stories (1991)

Partial Payments: Essays on Writers and Their Lives (1988)

Once More Around the Block: Familiar Essays (1987)

Plausible Prejudices: Essays on American Writing (1985)

Middle of My Tether: Familiar Essays (1983)

Ambition: The Secret Passion (1980)

Familiar Territory: Observations on American Life (1979)

Divorced in America: Marriage in an Age of Possibility (1974)

The Novel,

Who Needs It?

~

An Essay

Joseph Epstein

New York • London

First American edition published in 2023 by Encounter Books, an activity of Encounter for Culture and Education, Inc., a nonprofit, tax-exempt corporation. Encounter Books website address: www.encounterbooks.com

Manufactured in the United States and printed on acid-free paper. The paper used in this publication meets the minimum requirements of ANSI/NISO Z39.48-1992 (R 1997) (*Permanence of Paper*).

FIRST AMERICAN EDITION

LIBRARY OF CONGRESS CATALOGING-IN-PUBLICATION DATA

Names: Epstein, Joseph, 1937– author.
Title: The novel, who needs it? / Joseph Epstein.
Description: First American edition. | New York, New York: Encounter Books, 2023. | Includes bibliographical references and index.
Identifiers: LCCN 2022020638 (print) | LCCN 2022020639 (ebook)
ISBN 9781641773058 (cloth; acid-free paper) | ISBN 9781641773065 (ebook)
Subjects: LCSH: Fiction—History and criticism—Theory, etc.
Classification: LCC PN3331 .E67 2023 (print) | LCC PN3331 (ebook)
DDC 809.3—dc23/eng/20220721
LC record available at https://lccn.loc.gov/2022020638
LC ebook record available at https://lccn.loc.gov/2022020639

1 2 3 4 5 6 7 8 9 20 23

For Gary Fisher
Philosopher, Gambler, Good Guy

A great obstacle to good education is the inordinate passion prevalent for novels, and the time lost in that reading which should be instructively employed. When this poison infects the mind, it destroys its tone and revolts it against wholesome reading. Reason and fact, plain and unadorned, are rejected. Nothing can engage attention unless dressed in all the figments of fancy, and nothing so bedecked comes amiss. The result is a bloated imagination, sickly judgment, and disgust towards all the real businesses of life. This mass of trash, however, is not without some distinction; some few modelling their narratives, although fictitious, on the incidents of real life, have been able to make them interesting and useful vehicles of a sound morality.

—THOMAS JEFFERSON
Letter to Nathaniel Burwell (March 14, 1818)

I am man alive, and as long as I can, I intend to go on being man alive.... For this reason I am a novelist. And being a novelist, I consider myself superior to the saint, the scientist, the philosopher, and the poet, who are all great masters of different bits of man alive, but never get the whole hog.

—D. H. LAWRENCE
"Why the Novel Matters" (1936)

CONTENTS

∾

The Novel,

Who Needs It?

~

An Essay

I.

MANY YEARS AGO I heard that the writer Irving Kristol, in his day always a fount of good sense, had advised young people never to go into a job interview carrying a novel. Carrying a novel, his reasoning was, might suggest you are a touch frivolous—a lightweight and unserious, if not fundamentally unsound. Strikes me, this, as sensible advice.

This assumes, of course, that the person interviewing you is himself a bit, perhaps more than a bit, of a philistine, someone who doesn't mind telling you he never reads fiction, but instead, to establish his own intellectual credentials, reads only biographies and works on American history. In his view there figures to be something a touch airy-fairy about fiction, immature if not childish, harkening back to the day when you asked your mother to tell you a story before going to sleep. Such people are likely also to say that truth is stranger than fiction.

Truth may well be stranger than fiction, but, as the English novelist and screenwriter Frederic Raphael once noted, fiction is truer. By "truer" I believe Raphael meant that fiction—solid, serious, penetrating fiction—cuts deeper than such standard versions of truth-telling as those on offer in history, biography, social science, philosophy, and elsewhere. Grand claims, these, one might think, yet I happen to believe them. So apparently did Bernard

Malamud, in whose novel *The Assistant* the following bit of dialogue appears:

> He asked her what book she was reading.
> "*The Idiot*, do you know it?"
> "No. What's it about?"
> "It's a novel."
> "I'd rather read the truth," he said.
> "It is the truth."

The truth she is referring to is the truth of the imagination.

T. S. Eliot said of Henry James, perhaps the most thoughtful of
all students of fiction as well as among its most subtle practitioners,
that "he had a mind so fine no idea could violate it." Eliot meant
that James, in his novels and stories, operated above the realm of
ideas. In this realm a different kind of truth prevails—the truth of
the human heart. Marcel Proust, who with *In Search of Lost Time*
wrote easily the most elaborate and psychologically penetrating
single work in the long history of the novel, formulates this point
with characteristic insight when he writes:

> Our intellect is not the most subtle, the most powerful, the most
> appropriate, instrument for revealing the truth. It is life that,
> little by little, example by example, permits us to see that what is
> most important to our heart, or to our mind, is learned not by
> reasoning but through other agencies. Then it is that the intel-
> lect, observing their superiority, abdicates its control to them
> upon reasoned grounds, and agrees to become their collaborator
> and lackey.

Among these agencies are our feelings, sentiments, instincts,
promptings of conscience. Prominent among the ways that we
learn what is important to our heart and mind both, "little by little,

example by example," is through the reading of superior fiction. Apart from those who insist on a literal reading of it, the Bible itself may be viewed as a great novel, perhaps the greatest ever written, with its first part, The Old Testament, a grand family-chronicle novel, the second part, The New Testament, a picaresque, or work dominated by the adventures of a single hero.

Reading superior novels—novels by Cervantes, Jane Austen, Balzac, Tolstoy, Dickens, Dostoyevsky, George Eliot, Stendhal, Proust, Robert Musil, Willa Cather, and others—arouses the mind in a way that nothing else quite does. Some argue that the great advantage that novels have over other literary forms is that one can identify with the characters in them. One does indeed often make such identifications—wishing some fictional characters good fortune, yearning for their return to the story, sympathizing with their plights. One can also come to loathe characters in fiction for their hypocrisy, weakness, stupidity, malice. Perhaps no other literary form allows for such emotional engagement as does the novel. This notion of identification, this sense of participation in the plot and action of novels, may well be what entices many, especially many among the young, to read and take a deep pleasure in novels.

The novel at the top of its game of course provides more than the companionable emotion of literary identification. The genre, unlike any other literary genre, provides truths of an important kind unavailable elsewhere in literature or anywhere else. What these truths are I hope to set out over the course of this brief book.❡

II.

VLADIMIR NABOKOV, himself among the subtlest of modern novelists, thought that, if identify one must while reading a novel, the one best to identify with is the novel's author. Nabokov meant that the most sophisticated reading of a novel entails wondering why the novelist has done what he has, worrying about his manipulating his plot successfully, trying to determine how his mind works—in other words, putting yourself in the place of the novelist.

On this point the critic Percy Lubbock in *The Craft of Fiction* (1921) held that "there is nothing more that can usefully be said about a novel until we have fastened upon the question of its making and explored it to some purpose." By "identifying" with the author of a novel, we soon become acquainted with the technical aspects of the novel—why its author chose a first- rather than a third-person narrator, decided not to dramatize certain important scenes, supplied detail in some places and withheld it in others, and much else—and are thus able to read the novel more deeply, and thereby also be able, in Lubbock's words, "clearly and accurately" to understand the novel. By doing so, he adds, "the hours of the author's labor are lived again by the reader, the pleasure of creation is renewed."

We read novels and short stories differently than we read other prose works. If one reads a biography of, say, the Austrian

diplomatist Klemens von Metternich and comes across the three
goals he wished to achieve at the Congress of Vienna, one feels one
needs to make a mental note about those three goals, somehow
to be responsible for knowing what they were and why they were
significant. Characters in novels rarely have such clear-cut ambitions, goals, views. Even if they do, the novels in which they appear
are less about their achieving these goals than about life's manifold
ways of complicating their fate. In relation to their characters, serious novelists are themselves mini-gods, instructing these characters—and us with them—that life is more complex than they, and
perhaps we with them, ever imagined. Good novels are always
informing us that life is more various, richer, more surprising,
more bizarre than we had thought.

In a brilliant 1978 essay called "On Reading Books: A
Barbarian's Cogitations," Alexander Gerschenkron, then a labor
economist at Harvard, set out three criteria for a good book, a category that for him included novels. "A good book," Gerschenkron
wrote, "must be (1) interesting, (2) memorable, and (3) re-readable." As sensible as these three criteria are, so are they just that
unhelpful, at least from the standpoint of informing a person what
he or she ought to read. One cannot, of course, know if a book
is interesting until one has read it, nor if it is memorable until a
length of time has passed after one has read it, nor if it is worthy
of being reread until later in life one finds both the need and the
time to reread it. Gerschenkron's criteria, then, are a useful gauge
to judge the quality of what one has already read and quite useless
as a guide to what one ought to read. Still, one has to admire a man
who claims—and I have no doubt of the truth of the claim—to
have read *War and Peace* at least fifteen times, and twice "starting
again after having read the last page," so little did he want to depart
the rich world Leo Tolstoy had created in that magnificent, that
perhaps greatest of all novels.

Which brings me to the matter of rereading. Re-readability
is not only a useful criterion for a novel's worth, but such is the

complexity of serious novels that the same novel often reads differently at different ages while other novels cannot be read beyond a certain age and still others ought not to be read until one has attained to a later age. In this connection the Italian novelist Italo Calvino has described a classic as "a book that never finishes saying what it has to say."

I shall never forget as a young man having been swept up by John Dos Passos's trilogy *U.S.A.* (comprising *The 42nd Parallel*, *1919*, and *The Big Money*). I can even remember where I read large chunks of the work (on my stomach on the grass at nineteen in Indian Boundary Park on the far north side of Chicago). The trilogy, whose theme is injustice in American life and how it affects people's lives, was for the apolitical young man I then was an eye-opener. My admiration for its author, whose novels' scope took in all of the United States, was boundless. Nineteen, perhaps a bit earlier, was the perfect time to read *U.S.A.* Thirty may have been too late. I never attempted to reread the book, a work that John Dos Passos himself doubtless could not bear to reread, since all his political ideas underwent a radical change after his return from the Spanish Civil War when he discovered the murderous malevolence of international communism.

Around the same age, nineteen or twenty, I first read Ernest Hemingway's *The Sun Also Rises*, which is generally thought to be his major work. Here again I found myself greatly admiring the novel, feeling not a little envy for the panache of the expatriate generation presented in its pages. Twenty years later, now a university teacher, I attempted to teach *The Sun Also Rises* and found the novel not only difficult to get through but at different points laughable in its pretensions and unpleasant in its anti-Semitism. For my amusement while struggling through it I began marking the number of drinks the novel's characters consumed in its pages, stopping as I recall at seventy-nine around page 108. Ernest Hemingway's novel clearly failed, at least for me, the re-readability test.

With these two novelists in mind, Dos Passos and Hemingway, I have thought that perhaps novels, like movies, ought to carry codes suggesting the best age to read them: Hemingway and Dos Passos, LT (Late Teens); Aldous Huxley and F. Scott Fitzgerald, NAT (Not After Thirty); Marcel Proust and Robert Musil, NBF (Not Before Forty). Others' novels—those of Henry Miller, Philip Roth, Norman Mailer—would of course get an X rating.

The best novels and stories change along with their readers, and they get better upon rereading later in life. In *The Lyttelton Hart-Davis Letters*, the editor Rupert Hart-Davis writes to his former Eton master George Lyttelton that he has just reread Thornton Wilder's *The Bridge of San Luis Rey*, which he first read thirty-three years earlier, when he was twenty. He reports that "to my astonishment I now think it *first-rate*—a shaped and finished work of art—contrived, admittedly, but none the worse for that. . . . It seems to me to have improved and mellowed in thirty-three years, and I don't see why it shouldn't be read and enjoyed as long as books are read." Lyttelton replies by noting that rereading is "on the whole one of life's greatest pleasures."

Among the novelists I have reread with pleasure are Tolstoy and Proust, Jane Austen and George Eliot, Chekhov and Joseph Roth, Max Beerbohm and Willa Cather, Edith Wharton and Evelyn Waugh, Marguerite Yourcenar, and V. S. Naipaul, and a few others. Novelists whom I have felt no need to reread include Thomas Pynchon, Joseph Heller, J. D. Salinger, Jack Kerouac, John Barth, Kurt Vonnegut, Joyce Carol Oates, William Gaddis, and John Cheever. To have written a novel or stories that can be read twenty, fifty, a hundred, or four hundred years after its composition and can also be reread at different stages of a reader's life, is of course an extraordinary accomplishment. Señor Cervantes, take a bow. ❡

III.

MEMORY WORKS DIFFERENTLY in reading fiction than in other works, even to the point of sometimes scarcely working at all. I don't believe that we remember the details of novels in the same way that we might remember, say, a book on the history of British philosophy or another on movie musicals. Nor, I believe, are we called upon to do so. Yet odd details do stay in the mind. In Tolstoy's story "Father Sergius," for example, I recall how the eponymous character's finger twirled in the air before him when he chopped it off to avert sexual temptation. In one of Henry Miller's *Tropic* novels, the always down-at-the-heel Miller-like protagonist is making love to a woman standing up in a hallway, when her purse falls to the floor and a coin rolls out. "I made a mental note," the character notes, "to pick it up later." In Willa Cather's *Death Comes for the Archbishop*, I remember the soup served to the bishop by Blanchet, the priest who accompanies him on his travels into the new world of America, of which the bishop says, "… a soup like this is not the work of one man. It is the result of a constantly refined tradition. There are nearly a thousand years of history in this soup."

Here is a letter that touches on my point that appeared in the August 9, 2019, issue of the London *Times Literary Supplement*:

Sir,— I enjoyed the various reviews of Iris Murdoch in your
recent issue (July 12). I have read a good many of her novels,
some more than once. However, I wonder if other readers share
my experience. While reading an Iris Murdoch novel I am completely captivated, thoroughly within the world she has created.
No other writer I can think of has quite this effect. Yet, two days
later I couldn't tell you a thing about it. Enchantment?

> Richard Bachmann, Burlington,
> Ontario

I share Mr. Bachmann's experience, if not with the novels of
Iris Murdoch, of which I've read only a few and not much enjoyed
them, but with other novels and novelists. I am an admirer of the
novels of Barbara Pym, all of which I have read with much pleasure. I have written in praise of Miss Pym on two separate occa-
sions, but if you ask me today what happens in her novels *Excellent
Women* or *A Glass of Blessings*, I could not tell you. I have read
Dostoyevsky's *The Idiot* twice, yet all I can recall about it today is its
hero, Prince Myshkin, a saintly naïf who suffers, like Dostoyevsky,
from epilepsy. I could name other authentically splendid, and a few
great, novels I have read whose plots I can scarcely recall. ("He's
lost the plot," Australians say about people who are demented or
otherwise out of it.) Ought I to feel foolish about this? Does my
remembering little of what went on in these books mean that I
have wasted my time, all those hours of reading with nothing to
show for it?

I was pleased to find confirmation of my condition—and perhaps yours as well—in the pages of *The Craft of Fiction*, where Percy
Lubbock writes:

> Nothing, no power, will keep a book steady before us, so that
> we may have time to examine its shape and design. As quickly
> as we read it, it melts and shifts in the memory; even at the

moment when the last page is turned, a great part of the book, its finer detail, is already vague and doubtful. A little later, after a few days or months, how much is really left of it? A cluster of impressions, some clear points emerging from a mist of uncertainty, this is all we can hope to possess, generally speaking, in the name of a book.

While I can produce no hard evidence that I read many novels whose plots now escape me, I nonetheless walk the streets as a man who has read all the novels of Barbara Pym, *The Idiot* (twice), and many other novels in which I have lost significant details of their fascinating characters' lives. How was it, again, that Dickens's wonderful Mr. Micawber ended up? What eventually happened to Dostoyevsky's Nikolai Stavrogin in *The Possessed*? At the close of *Madame Bovary*, Monsieur Homais, the hypocritical Yonville pharmacist, receives the cross of the Legion of Honor, but just how did Charles Bovary take his own life? I do not worry overmuch about having lost the plots of novels—even of superior novels—because I am confident that they have nonetheless left a rich deposit in my mind of a kind that, I like to believe, goes well beyond recollecting the details of their plots.

This deposit is in part a considerable broadening of my experience. The broadening takes place in various realms. I have read histories of the Napoleonic wars, but the genius of Leo Tolstoy, in his battle sections of *War and Peace*, has put me in those wars in ways no straight historical account—numbering casualties, discussing strategy, toting up geo-political significance—can hope to do. The *belle époque* of late nineteenth-century France, including much about it that was a great deal less than *belle*, is nowhere better on view than in Marcel Proust's *In Search of Lost Time*. The peculiar feeling of displacement and yet dignity that accompanies the immigrant experience in America is on display nowhere more vividly than in the novels and stories of Willa Cather. While I may not be able to report back in detail all I have learned from them, these and other novels have enriched my own experience in countless ways.

In skillful hands, the novel can give us greater insight into history than history itself does. One could, for example, put together a list of novels that would tell more about the history and psychological condition of the United States than a general history of the subject. For me this list would include *The Last of the Mohicans, The Scarlet Letter, Uncle Tom's Cabin, Moby-Dick, The Red Badge of Courage, The Portrait of a Lady, McTeague, Sister Carrie, The Great Gatsby, My Ántonia, An American Tragedy, Main Street,* the *Snopes* trilogy, *Native Son,* the *Rabbit* novels.

The knowledge—and with luck occasional touches of wisdom—that one acquires through reading novels differs from that acquired reading history, biography, science, criticism, scholarship, and all else. For one thing, it is less exact; for another it has no use outside itself. The knowledge provided by the best novels is knowledge that cannot be enumerated nor subjected to strict testing. Wider, less confined, deeper, its subject is human existence itself, in all its dense variousness and often humbling confusion. Reading great novels comports well with the best definition of education I know, that set out by the poet and Eton master William Johnson Cory (1823–92), which runs:

> A certain amount of knowledge you can indeed with average faculties acquire so as to retain; nor need you regret the hours you spent on much that is forgotten, for the shadow of lost knowledge at least protects you from many illusions. But you go to a great school [I would insert here "you read great novels"] not so much for knowledge as for art and habits; for the habit of attention, for the art of expression, for the art of assuming at a moment's notice a new intellectual position, for the art of entering quickly into another person's thoughts, for the habit of

submitting to censure and refutation, for the art of indicating assent or dissent in graduated terms, for the habit of regarding minute points of accuracy, for the art of working out what is possible in a given time, for taste, for discrimination, for mental courage, and for mental soberness. ❡

IV.

PLOT, OF COURSE, is what hooks one in a novel, engaging one's own emotions with the destiny of its characters. E. M. Forster distinguishes between a story and a plot, with causality being the point of difference. "The king died and then the queen died is a story," he notes. "The king died, and then the queen died of grief is plot." Rupert Hart-Davis noted that "No narrative is any good unless you want to know what's going to happen [next]." Without an interesting plot, most novels have little right to exist, though not all even great novelists were adept at plotting—Flaubert for one, Dickens for another. Many of Dickens's novels were written to meet newspaper and magazine deadlines; he sometimes had two novels in composition at once, so it is scarcely surprising that his plots are often less than tightly strung. On the other hand, in *The Tale of Two Cities*, Charles Dickens wrote the best opening and closing sentences in all of fiction. The novel opens, it will be recalled:

> It was the best of times, it was the worst of times, it was the age of wisdom, it was the age of foolishness, it was the epoch of belief, it was the epoch of incredulity, it was the season of Light, it was the season of Darkness, it was the spring of hope, it was the winter of despair, we had everything before us, we had nothing before us, we were all going direct to Heaven, we were all

going direct the other way—in short, the period was so far like
the present period, that some of its noisiest authorities insisted
on its being received, for good or evil, in the superlative degree
of comparison only.

(Some might argue that Tolstoy's opening to *Anna Karenina*, "All
happy families are alike, but every unhappy family is unhappy
in its own way," is better, but I would reply that I don't believe all
happy families are alike, which takes much of the punch out of the
sentence.) And of course *A Tale of Two Cities* closes with Sydney
Carton, on his way to the guillotine, to sacrifice his life for that of
Charles Darnay, the husband of Lucie, his unrequiting lover: "It is a
far, far better thing I do, than I have ever done; it is a far, far better
rest that I go to than I have ever known."

Flaubert went so far as to disdain plot altogether. "The story,
the plot of a novel is of no interest to me," he wrote. "When I write
a novel I aim at rendering a color, a shade. For instance in my
Carthaginian novel [*Salammbô*], I want to do something purple."
(The plots of Shakespeare's plays, to digress slightly into drama, are
for the most part pathetic, when not preposterous; it is instead the
power and poetry of his language that carries his plays.) Gerard de
Nerval claimed that there existed only twenty-four different plots;
Goethe pushed the number up to thirty-six. The ability to tell a
story is but one aspect of the novelist's art, one part of his mission,
but it can be, and often is, crucial.

In his essay "The Art of Fiction," Henry James compared the
work of the novelist to that of the painter. Both, he contended, set
out to capture life. James writes: "A novel is in its broadest definition a personal, a direct impression of life: that, to begin with, constitutes its value, which is greater or less according to the intensity
of its impression." He adds: "A novel is a living thing, all one and
continuous, like any other organism, and in proportion as it lives
will it be found, I think, that in each of its parts there is something
of each of the other parts."

Henry James is especially good on the wide domain of the novel, whose province is all of experience, though he himself has been accused of concentrating in his own fiction on too narrow a slice of human experience, restricting the content of so much of his fiction to well-born, highly sentient men and women, and in *The Awkward Age* to a girl in late adolescence, and in *What Maisie Knew* to a highly precocious child.

A single novel can touch on the wildest adventure but also dwell on the most private personal psychology. Melville's *Moby-Dick* is an obvious example here. A novel can incorporate history, engage in philosophy, confront morality. Critics speak of novels of ideas, novels of character, psychological novels, historical novels, adventure novels—the novel can be all these things, but above all it is the book of life. More than any other literary form, the novel is best able to accommodate the messiness of detail that life presents. The novel, for those who love it, is the literary form of forms.

"Educated by Novels" is the title of an essay I wrote more than thirty years ago that attempted to make the case for reading novels by setting out their importance in my own education. As a student, I realized that I had no aptitude for science, that foreign languages did not come easily to me, and that the study of economics turned my eyeballs to isinglass. (As economics do to this day, when I can barely concentrate on statements about my own personal finances.) In literature, I adored much poetry but felt I could not draw intel-lectual breath for long on its high plateau; the drama—allowing for the magnificence of Euripides and Aeschylus, Shakespeare and Molière—was for me a form that always felt a touch artificial. But the novel, the novel from the very beginning—when as a boy I read *Hans Brinker, or the Silver Skates*, *Black Beauty*, and then the sports novels of John R. Tunis—the novel lit my fire and continues to light it today. The novel took me to places I hadn't known exist-ed, but in which I was delighted to find myself; it expanded my world like nothing else I had known, or, for that matter, still know. If bookish knowledge was to have value, and I never doubted that it did, the most valuable of such knowledge for me, I fairly early realized, was likely to be found in novels.

A reviewer's platitudinous compliment for a novel is to call it "a real page-turner." A "good read" is another such compliment. When young the facility, the ease, with which one could read a novel recommended it. I can remember, as a boy of sixteen, traveling with my father, staying up all night in Brown's Hotel in Des Moines, Iowa, to finish Willard Motley's *Knock on Any Door*, a real page-turner. ("Live fast, die young, and leave a good-looking corpse" is its hero Nick Romano's motto, which is all I remember about the novel today.) In the realm of novels, real page-turners tend to make good movies, which often turn out better than the novels themselves. The reason is that these page-turners tend to be all plot—little character, and less thought. Only later in life did it occur to me that in the realm of novels it wasn't page-turners I most admired, but what I thought of as page-stoppers— novels that made you want to stop to reread key passages, to admire brilliant formulations, to pause to grasp the import of the material, and to consider how the novelist had achieved his marvelous effects.

Many years ago it was believed that movies would replace the novel (as later it was said television would replace the movies, and today that digital culture will replace both). Like novels, movies are a form that relies on narrative, but the watching of movies differs from the reading of novels in substantive ways. For one, watching a movie is a much more passive activity than reading a novel. For another, movies have nowhere the same power of entering into a character's thoughts as do novels. As the novelist Allan Massie has written: "Film hasn't superseded the novel. As a medium for examining the way we live and the way we should live, film has for the most part proved wretchedly inadequate. Its ability to explore moral or ethical questions is slight, because such exploration must be verbal, and film deals in images. Film is a great simplifier; that is part of its charm." Despite *auteur* theory, holding that the true author of a movie is its director, movies are the work of many hands—director, actors, cameramen, editors, technicians—while novels are unitary in their vision. Despite all that recommend movies—they can be influential, delightful, touch on the significant—they cannot hope to command the depth of perception that the best novels achieve.

Forty or so years ago, movies appeared to have been the artwork of the age. At social gatherings among the middle and upper-middle classes, the popular movie of the day was often topic number one. One felt under an obligation to have seen the most recent movies, and not only to have seen them and formed an opinion about them, but to have known what Andrew Sarris, John Simon, Richard Schickel, Pauline Kael, and other movie critics of the day thought about them. The movies of European directors—Truffaut, Fellini, Antonioni, Godard, Renoir, Resnais—were thought to qualify as high art, and thus allowed those who went to their movies the added thrill of believing that they were themselves participating in high culture. Older American movies were declared classics, and had full-blown books written about them. Was this overkill? Someone who thought so was Julius Epstein, who with his brother Philip wrote the screenplay for *Casablanca*, a movie about which full-blown books have been written. When an admirer told Julius Epstein what a magnificent work of art *Casablanca* is, Epstein, with a nice sense of measure, is said to have replied, "Yea, it's a pretty slick piece of shit."

To return to Henry James's analogy between the novelist and painter, in a good novel plot is for the novelist what canvas is for the painter: the surface on which the real subject is displayed. With his strict insistence on form, James put down the great Russian novels of the nineteenth century as "baggy monsters." James was wrong. Baggy they may well be, but monstrous not in the least; they are instead works that, in the power of their treatment of the grandest subject matter, surmount and surpass the need for formal perfection.

An essay, perhaps a small book, could be written on the subject of great writers misjudging other great writers. Along with Henry James on the Russians, perhaps the most notable instance of this is Tolstoy's low view of Shakespeare, set out in an essay he wrote attacking Shakespeare as an "inartistic, insignificant writer" whose "works do not satisfy the demands of all art, and, besides this, their tendency is of the lowest and most immoral." One of my favorite literary anecdotes, recounted in Henri Troyat's splendid biography of Tolstoy, has Tolstoy and Chekhov in conversation at Gaspra, in the Crimea, when Tolstoy turns to the younger Chekhov to tell him how much he admires his stories, encouraging him to write more and more stories. "But your plays, Anton Pavlovich, your plays, my dear fellow, are sorry things, wanting in so many ways, your plays are really poor stuff, worse even than Shakespeare." ¶

V.

THE WORD "NOVEL" suggests that the true subject of the form is what is new—or, as is sometimes said, the novel brings the news. What news might this be? Anthony Trollope wrote a novel with the title *The Way We Live Now*, which is one answer. Such a title, of course, implicitly prompts the question, who, exactly, is "we"? More often than not, people have read novels to learn not how they themselves but how other people live or have lived: royalty, or aristocrats, or social classes below or above one's own. When I, a middle-class kid, was in high school, I went on a brief jag of reading novels about working-class, somewhat thuggish youth—*A Stone for Danny Fisher*, *The Amboy Dukes*, *The Hoods*, *Knock on Any Door*—partly to understand, and partly to be titillated by, how what I took to be the lower classes lived. Other novelists have brought us news not of how we lived but how we shall one day live. I am not thinking here of science fiction, for which I have never felt the least affinity, but instead of Franz Kafka, whose novels anticipate the bureaucratic, even totalitarian future that was, in Kafka's own day, so near at hand.

Closer to our day, Tom Wolfe, who began life as a journalist, in mid-career turned to the novel and wrote penetratingly about the way we live now. In *The Bonfire of the Vanities*, he wrote about the newly rich glitterati of Manhattan; in *A Man in Full* he gave us an inside view of the world of real estate moguls and bankers in

23

Atlanta, Georgia, with a side trip to life in prison; in *I Am Charlotte Simmons*, he chronicled the sex and other shenanigans that are carried on in the contemporary university. These novels found a large audience, and when put down by John Updike, Norman Mailer, and John Irving as little more than best-sellers, Wolfe responded by reminding them that "Shakespeare, Balzac, Dickens, Dostoyevsky, Tolstoy, Gogol, Zola, Ibsen, and Shaw, not to mention Mark Twain, all of whom were enormously popular in their own day…all would have been highly amused by the attempt to place literature here on this side of the fence and entertainment and popularity there on the other."

If any criticism is to be made of Tom Wolfe's fiction, it is perhaps that it is too heavily journalistic. His penchant was for realism in the novel, and his own novels bring great quantities of information about the way people live and work and about their own (usually empty) ambitions. Too often he provides details well beyond what the novel requires. In *The Bonfire of the Vanities*, for example, the attire of his characters is elaborately described along with the name brands of these clothes, where they were purchased, and what they cost. Wolfe's novels tend to disappoint in the realm of character. His characters feel flat—they do not, in E. M. Forster's definition of "round" characters, "surprise"—they fail to gain by their experiences, they contribute little to helping unravel the puzzle that is life for the rest of us. Yet in response to his writer-critics, Tom Wolfe was not mistaken when he wrote that by "turning their backs on the rich material of an amazing country at a fabulous moment in its history," those writers lost "reality, the pulse of the human beast," the great subject of the novel, which is life itself.

The novel, then, is about the new in a more profound way than bringing the news of how people live. In *The Rise of the Novel* (1957) Ian Watt makes the point that the primary criterion of the novel from its origins in the early eighteenth century "was truth to individual experience—individual experience which is always unique and therefore new." Watt goes on to note: "from the Renaissance onwards, there was a growing tendency for individual experience to replace collective tradition as the ultimate arbiter of reality; and this transition would seem to constitute an important part of the general cultural background of the novel." The novel, in other words, was new in its reliance on originality of experience and its concentration on individual experience; its characters and their story, had to be fresh, striking, original. Each novel was under the obligation to be itself novel.

Novels can contain poetry and philosophy in ways that neither philosophy nor poetry quite do. I write "the novel," but of course there are novels, all sorts of novels, all with different appeals to different persons. In *The Art of the Novel* (1986), Milan Kundera mentions four different "appeals" of the novel: the appeal of play, or playfulness (examples include Laurence Sterne's *Tristram Shandy* and Denis Diderot's *Jacques le Fataliste*, as well as many of the stories of Jorge Luis Borges), the appeal of dream (Kafka is Kundera's leading practitioner here), the appeal of thought (he cites Robert Musil and Hermann Broch, and I would add Thomas Mann and Saul Bellow), and the appeal of time (Proust, pre-eminently). What all have in common is the attempt to grasp and cage that elusive bird known as reality.¶

VI.

MANY OF THE MOST interesting minds of the modern age, though not themselves literary figures, have taken much pleasure and, it is not going too far to say, intellectual sustenance from novels. The economist John Maynard Keynes, the philosopher José Ortega y Gasset, the jurist Oliver Wendell Holmes, Jr., the political scientist Michael Oakeshott, the sociologist Edward Shils, and the anthropologist Clifford Geertz were devoted readers of novels—all men who, in their own writings, seemed to transcend their own intellectual and scholarly specialties. (The English philosopher Gilbert Ryle, when asked if he read novels, answered, "Yes—all six," by which he meant the six novels of Jane Austen, which one gathers he read over and over.) What was it, do you suppose, that these men, towering intellectuals all, found in novels that they couldn't find in economics, philosophy, jurisprudence, political science, sociology, and anthropology?

What such impressive intellectual figures found in novels, I believe, is a respect for the complexity of experience unavailable anywhere else. In 1930 Justice Holmes wrote to Harold Laski that he had just read "what seems to me a really great novel, *My Ántonia*—by Willa Cather—turning the life of early settlers on the prairie (in our time), so hard, so squalid, into a noble poem. I do like an author who doesn't have to go to London or Paris or Vienna to find his genius—but realizes that any part of the universe can be seen poetically and takes what he finds at hand and makes it blossom."

Concepts have their value, but they tend to explain more than they can justify. From Karl Marx's class-struggle to Max Weber's linking the rise of capitalism to the rise of Protestantism to Sigmund Freud's Oedipus Complex, conceptual thinking tends invariably to be both overly ambitious and sketchy, leaving out crucial aspects of human experience, and thereby necessarily highly simplifying. "Create a concept," Ortega wrote, "and reality leaves the room." Scientists, historians, politicians, economists, and poets all perceived the world, as Michael Oakeshott noted, through what he termed their separate "mode of experience," but for him each of these modes was partial, incomplete, only part of the story. Oakeshott also felt that the whole story was not to be encompassed through any discrete mode of learning, even through philosophy, with its pretensions to be architectonic. He never mentions that one mode, the novel, where the whole story can be at least attempted.

Milan Kundera, himself the author of such novels as *The Unbearable Lightness of Being*, *The Joke*, and *The Farewell Waltz*, defines the novel as "the great prose form in which an author thoroughly explores, by means of experimental selves (characters), some great themes of existence." The novel for Kundera is and always has been "a meditation on human existence," and the novelist is above all "an explorer of existence." Discovery, for Kundera, is one of the chief functions of the novel.

In *Aspects of the Novel* (1927), E. M. Forster, after quoting Abel Chevalley's bland definition of the novel as "a fiction in prose of a certain extent," adds that it is "any fictitious prose work over 50,000 words." Forster allows the difficulty of coming up with a satisfying definition of a genre that includes such disparate works as *The Pilgrim's Progress*, *Marius the Epicurean*, *The Adventures of a Younger Son*, *The Magic Flute*, *A Journal of the Plague Year*, *Zuleika*

Dobson, Rasselas, Ulysses, and *Green Mansions.* For him what all
novelists have in common is "to reveal the hidden life at its source:
to tell us more about Queen Victoria than could be known [by the
historian], and thus to produce a character who is not the Queen
Victoria of history."

Much earlier Samuel Johnson defined the novel as "a small
tale, generally about love," though this was before Samuel
Richardson, in his novels *Pamela* and *Clarissa*, greatly expanded
the length and especially the depth of novelistic love stories. Closer
to our own time, Ford Madox Ford defined the novel as "a printed
book of some length telling one tale or relating the adventures
of one single personage." The *Oxford Dictionary*, somewhat awk-
wardly, defines the novel as "a fictitious prose narrative of sufficient
length to fill one or more volumes, portraying characters and
actions representative of real life in a continuous plot." The vexing
problem of defining the novel is almost enough to make one accept
Randall Jarrell's amusing definition of the novel as "a prose narrative of some length that has something wrong with it," and let it go
at that.

What truly interests the novelist, in Kundera's words, is "the
paradoxical nature of action" and the "role the irrational plays in
our decisions in our own lives." The novelist explores these through
his characters, and for Kundera a character only comes alive when
the novelist gets "to the bottom of his existential problem." The
problem, in the best of novels, is one fraught with complexity as
the character works his way through what Kundera refers to as
"the trap" that is life. "That life is a trap," Kundera told an interviewer from the *Paris Review*, "we've always known: we are born
without having been asked to be, locked in body we never chose,
and destined to die." Joseph Conrad spells this out in fuller scope:
"The pursuit of happiness by means lawful and unlawful, through
resignation or revolt, by the clever manipulation of conventions or
by the solemn hanging to the skirts of the latest scientific theory,

is the only theme that can be legitimately developed by the novelist, who is the chronicler of the adventures of mankind among the
dangers of the kingdom of the earth."

If the novel is an instrument of discovery, what it sets out to
discover are bits of that still unsolvable and greatest of all great
mysteries, human nature. The philosopher John Gray, in his book
Feline Philosophy, writes that human nature "is expressed in the
universal demand for meaning, for one thing. But human nature
has produced many divergent and at times antagonistic forms of
life. How can anyone know their own nature, when human nature
is so contradictory?" One place to look is into one's own heart,
another is in great literature. "For any detailed description of the
complexity of human nature," wrote Beatrice Webb, "I had to turn
to novelists and poets."

What truly moves human beings? What is the force behind our
actions good and bad, behind hatred, love, loyalty, betrayal? What
is it in us that gives rise to optimism, pessimism, cynicism, cheer-
fulness? Is morality innate or only learned through religion? Why
do those who in their actions abandon self-preservation excite our
admiration? What truly constitutes good character? Perhaps the
difference between human beings and animals is not alone that
human beings have what is called propositional speech, or the
ability to speak and think in sentences, but that humans, unlike
most animals, are inconsistent, for inconsistency, too, is part of our
nature. These and so many other large questions are behind the
never-ending quest to understand that mystery of mysteries—the
mystery that, millennia after millennia, still remains a mystery:
human nature.

The novel has worked at the answers to these questions more
persistently than any other artistic form or intellectual endeavor.
However circumstances and conditions may change, the great
questions surrounding human nature do not. As Kundera writes,
the "light that radiates from the great novels time can never dim,

for human existence is perpetually being forgotten by man, and thus the novelists' discoveries, however old they may be, will never cease to astonish us." Not that the novel has answered all the questions about human nature—clearly it has not—but what at its best it has done is formulate and highlight those questions more successfully than anywhere else.

The spirit of the novel entails questioning, complexity, irony, dubiety about much that others consider home truths. The writing of fiction is an act of testing. I have not myself written a novel, but I have published fifty or so short stories, and in the writing of these stories I have found my own beliefs regularly tested—and, in the creation of fictional characters, sometimes found these same beliefs sadly wanting. Those beliefs that fall by the wayside, though they once seemed sensible enough, do not account for the often paradoxical, not to say irrational, behavior of human beings, both inside novels and stories and out in the world. The writing of fiction calls upon a different kind of thought than does philosophy and other modes of intellectual endeavor and ratiocination. Kundera notes that Dostoyevsky, a man whose quotidian life was wrecked by gambling and was a shambles generally, who was an anti-Semite and harbored other foolish ideas, this same Dostoyevsky "is a great thinker *only* [my italics] as a novelist."

What made Fyodor Dostoyevsky a great thinker is the method of the novel. The greatest Russian thinkers, as the critic and Slavicist Gary Saul Morson has noted, have always been the nation's novelists. And this because they, the Russian novelists, put the abstraction of ideas to the test of plausibility through their characters and the exigencies of the plots they put these characters through. In a brilliant reading of *The Brothers Karamazov*, Morson argues that this novel not only demonstrates "a Christian understanding of life," but refutes the arguments against Christianity by demolishing the atheist notions that "all is permitted, wishes have no moral value, and only active participants [in acts of human

viciousness] are morally responsible," while also offering "the
deepest understanding of ethics and psychology available."
That a number of novelists turn out to be more intelligent
in their books than in their persons is a paradox of great interest. The method of the novel makes this possible. At the heart
of this method is the hypothetical posing of questions—chiefly
moral questions—through the lives of imagined characters. And
character, as Aristotle puts it in *The Poetics*, "is that which reveals
moral purpose." For me the most serious, the most significant,
the best novels are those through whose pages a never blatant, if
not always obvious, but ultimately central moral conflict plays out
and is generally resolved. In an essay called "Prosaics," Gary Saul
Morson writes that in the novels of Leo Tolstoy and others "we
see moral decisions made moment by moment by inexhaustibly
complex characters in unrepeatable social situations at particular
historical times; and we see that the value of these decisions cannot be abstracted from these specifics." Through the reading of
serious novels, Morson contends, "one's sense of moral complexity
is enriched. Such enrichment is essential to moral education and
is in principle endless. A moral resting point is never earned once
and for all."

The major religions, however valuable their moral instruction,
cannot hope entirely to cover the vast waterfront of moral con-
frontations that life, that gremlinesque trickster, continues to set in
our paths. I cannot resist setting out here the example of a friend,
long divorced from his bi-polar wife, whom the trickster put to a
tough test. This woman, long after her marriage to my friend, had a
child out of wedlock with a man who took no responsibility for the
child. The seven-year-old child meanwhile was raised with various deleterious ideas: medicine and dentistry are harmful, schools
wish only to indoctrinate you in bad ideas, and more. At one point
this woman abused the child, who was taken from her by the state
Child Protection Service, which planned to place him in foster

homes. My friend had laid out in his mind careful plans for his recent retirement. But now, confronted with the bleak future likely for this child in foster care, a child who is no blood relation to him but the half-brother of his own children, he felt he had no choice but to step in and raise the child on his own, which he will spend the better part of the next decade doing, thereby dashing all his plans for his leisurely retirement. He did the right thing, the noble thing even, but the moral of the story is clear: Want to make God smile? Tell Him your plans. Indeed, "Want to make God smile? Tell Him your plans" might well serve as the motto for the novelist.⸙

VII.

GIVEN—AND NO SMALL "GIVEN" IS IT—a novelist's ability to make his characters come alive, he must then direct their action in his novel. In making choices for them, he must take into consideration the vast realm of possibilities consistent with human nature as he understands it. If his characters make only rational, sensible, chiefly conventional choices, he will likely have written an immensely dull book. Neither logic nor good sense will necessarily guide the behavior of characters in novels; instead the congeries of misapprehensions, mistaken motives, misreadings of the characters of others, and more in the same human, all-too-human line that, taken together, go by the name of reality, must be taken into account and duly described in the successful novel.

Such is the force of novelistic method, the novelist himself sometimes changes his view of his own characters midway in the composition of his novel. The most famous instance of this is Tolstoy in *Anna Karenina*. Tolstoy set out despising Anna, considering her a fashionable, frivolous, feckless female, undeserving of the least sympathy. Then in mid-composition, he seems, through the mystery of literary creation, to have fallen in love with her. No sooner did he do so than Anna takes on depth, gains our sympathy, becoming in the end a tragic figure, one of the great characters in all of literature.

In superior fiction, characters not only come alive but can over the years change in the minds of their readers. Consider Anna Karenina's husband, Alexei Alexandrovich Karenin. Should one happen to read *Anna Karenina* in one's youth, he, Karenin, seems a constricted, stuffy, wholly unimaginative man. Encountered later in life, he becomes a victim, a dignified figure deserving sympathy in a tragedy not of his own making. In her book *Proust and the Squid*, Maryanne Wolf writes about her later-life reading of George Eliot's character Edward Casaubon in *Middlemarch*: "I never thought I would see the day when I empathized with Mr. Casaubon, but now, with no small humility, I do. So also did George Eliot, perhaps for reasons similar to my own." Part of the great mystery of the novel is that not only do characters change but so do readers. As Maryanne Wolf nicely puts it: "Reading changes our lives, and our lives change our reading."

The novelist must also attend to the strange, always strong hand that fate plays upon his characters. In the realm of fate are such determinative aspects of life as the parents to whom these characters were born, the country and city and time in which they live, the aptitudes and skills they possess, and so much more. Fate, in literature as in life, is often the greatest, and not seldom the trickiest, of all plot makers. Plutarch, in his life of the Corinthian general Timoleon, remarks on "the strange dexterity of fortune's operations, the strange facility with which she makes one event the spring and motion to something wholly different, uniting every scattered accident and loose particular and remote action, and interweaving them together to serve her purpose; so that things in themselves that seem to have no connection or independence whatsoever, become in her hands, so to say, the end and the beginning of each other." Literature, wrote Isaac Bashevis Singer, "is the story of love and fate, a description of the mad hurricane of human passions and the struggle with them." Fate, in literature as in life, cannot be known or predicted. Yet, as Pindar had it, "Nor fire nor brazen wall can keep out fate."

To lapse briefly into autobiography, here is an example of the odd, twisted hand that fate has played in my own life. When I was in the peacetime Army, stationed at Fort Hood, Texas, I learned that a few jobs had become available for clerks in recruiting stations in Little Rock, Arkansas, and in Shreveport, Louisiana. I applied, and, lo, one morning was told that I had been selected for one of these clerkships. At the desk of the rather gruff staff sergeant who was assigning the jobs, I was asked which recruiting station I preferred, Little Rock or Shreveport. I sensed I had only a nano-second to reply. Perhaps because of its greater proximity to Chicago, where my parents and friends lived, I said, "Little Rock, Sergeant." And off to Little Rock I went. After six or so months there I met and soon after married my first wife (of two), with whom I had two sons.

How different would my life have been, I have often since wondered, if I had said, "Shreveport, Sergeant?" Fate—go figure.¶

VIII.

IF THE NOVEL HAS A HISTORY, it isn't necessarily one of unrelenting progress. The history of literature (and the arts generally), unlike that of science, isn't a tale of successive victories built on those that have gone before. Instead the history of the novel shows high periods and low, and the reasons for these rises and falls are not often easily explained. The Russian novelists of the nineteenth century—Gogol, Tolstoy, Dostoyevsky, Goncharov, Leskov, and finally Chekhov, who is of course more notable for his short stories—mark one of its pinnacles. The Victorians novelists—with Dickens, Thackeray, George Eliot, the Brontës, Anthony Trollope—mark another. Twentieth-century England would produce Evelyn Waugh, Anthony Powell, Kingsley Amis, Barbara Pym, Elizabeth Bowen, and others. The United States had a few good runs, first with James Fenimore Cooper, Nathaniel Hawthorne, Herman Melville, Henry James, and Mark Twain; later with Theodore Dreiser, F. Scott Fitzgerald, Ernest Hemingway, William Faulkner, and Willa Cather. Some would argue for another good run represented by Bernard Malamud, Saul Bellow, Norman Mailer, William Styron, and Philip Roth. No one can quite account for why or how these extraordinary peaks in the history of the novel came about when they did, apart from saying that certain talents, often very different kinds of talents, happened to emerge around the same time.

Another sort of history could be written around innovations in the novel. This might begin with *Don Quixote*, the splendidly comic creation of Cervantes' "knight of the doleful countenance," a book that is often cited as initiating the modern novel. Samuel Richardson would earn a place here among innovators for being the first to consider the interior thought of his characters. Henry Fielding brought irony into play. Daniel Defoe concentrated his interest on single—and singular—characters: Robinson Crusoe, Moll Flanders. Laurence Sterne in (*Tristram Shandy*) and Denis Diderot (in *Jacques le Fataliste*) playfully mocked the very notion of narrative. Flaubert and the French (and Turgenev along with them) wrote with the aesthetics of the novel much in mind. Emile Zola took up the fortunes of the working class under the aegis of realism. Kafka lent an aura of impersonal paranoia, leading onto fantasy. James Joyce introduced stream of consciousness. Saul Bellow and others produced *romans à clef*, or novels based fairly closely on living or recently dead people. Thomas Mann, Hermann Broch, and Robert Musil wrote fiction at whose core was the playing out of ideas through characters and plot and other of the conventional means of fiction. Such writers as Jorge Luis Borges and Vladimir Nabokov, international in their outlook, added a touch of the cosmopolitan, the supra-national, sensibility to fiction.

Of the various forms the novel has taken—the family chronicle, the picaresque, the satire, the novel of ideas—the last, the novel of ideas, may seem a contradiction. I say a contradiction because, first, while all serious novels are ultimately about ideas, the best novels always put facts before ideas. "It is the business of literature," as the critic Desmond MacCarthy once put it, "to turn facts into ideas." When ideas are at the forefront in fiction, when ideas dictate fact, characters seem diminished, plot suffers, and reality leaves not only the room but the novel. "An interest in ideas and theoretical statements," the critic Northrop Frye wrote, "is alien to the genius of the novel proper, where the technical problem is to dissolve all theory into personal relationships."

To be sure, novels are ultimately about ideas, but ideas played out in the lives of their characters. The great Russian novelists understood this and perhaps executed it best. "Novels of ideas usually examine theories not in terms of logical coherence, as philosophical treatises do," as Gary Saul Morson has put it, "but by showing what it means to live by them." Morson adds: "For Dostoyevsky, as for the other great Russian fiction writers, novels are not just forms in which ideas are expressed. They are themselves philosophical instruments."

In *Politics and the Novel* (1957), Irving Howe puts a different twist on the issue of ideas in fiction. Howe held that it was mistaken to believe "that abstract ideas invariably contaminate a work of art and should be kept at a safe distance from it. No doubt, when the armored columns of ideology troop *en masse*, they do imperil a novel's life and liveliness, but ideas, be they in free isolation or hooped into formal systems, are indispensable to the serious novel." The political novel is ultimately a novel of ideas, and, as Howe notes, "at its best, the political novel generates such intense heat that the ideas it appropriates are melted into its movement and fused with the emotions of its characters." Dostoyevsky's *The Possessed* is perhaps the best example of this fusion successfully executed.

Yet an author hostage to certain locked-in or coarse ideas can destroy a novel. Even though in most quarters it is taken for one among the greatest of novels, Flaubert's *Madame Bovary* is for me a case in point. Midway in an essay on Tolstoy's *Anna Karenina*, Matthew Arnold pauses to compare Tolstoy's novel to *Madame Bovary*, two novels with similar subjects, and finds the latter wanting. Over *Madame Bovary*, Arnold finds, "hangs an atmosphere of bitterness, irony, impotence; not a person in the book to rejoice or console us; the springs of freshness and feeling are not there to create such personages." While the trajectories of both novels, *Anna Karenina* and *Madame Bovary*, are similar—each is a story about the destructive wages of adultery—Emma Bovary lacks Anna Karenina's vivacity and charm, chiefly because, as Arnold notes, "the treasures of compassion, tenderness, insight, which alone, amid such guilt and misery, can enable charm to subsist and to emerge, are wanting to Flaubert." Flaubert, Arnold concludes, "is cruel, with the cruelty of petrified feeling, to his poor heroine; he pursues her without pity or pause, as with malignity; he is harder upon her himself than any reader ever, I think, will be inclined to be."

What was behind this "petrified feeling" in Flaubert? I believe it was an idea, the idea of the loathsomeness of the French bourgeoisie, of whom Charles and Emma Bovary are culled out as examples and thereby must, in the blaze of Flaubert's hatred of their social class, be consumed by the flame of this hatred. An idea—a coarse, empty idea—was at the wheel while Flaubert was writing his novel, and for Matthew Arnold, and for me along with him, spoiled it.

Ideas must be slowly digested within characters, as Jane Austen and Henry James well understand, and must not, as in Thomas Mann's *Magic Mountain*, be meant to represent them. I think Thomas Mann a great novelist, but I prefer him in his less ideational works: *Buddenbrooks* over *The Magic Mountain*, "Tonio Kröger," "Death in Venice," and other stories over *Dr. Faustus*. For an example of ideas presented directly in novels, here is a passage from the first volume of Hermann Broch's trilogy *The Sleepwalkers*:

> On the theme of the military uniform Bertrand could have supplied some such theory as this:
>> Once upon a time it was the Church alone that was exalted as judge over mankind, and every layman knew that he was a

sinner. Nowadays it is the layman who has to judge his fellow-
sinner if all values are not to fall into anarchy, and instead of
weeping with him, brother must say to brother: "You have
done wrong." And as once it was only the garments of the
priest that marked a man off from his fellows as something
higher, some hint of the layman peeping through even the
uniform and robe of office, so, when the great intolerance
of faith was lost, the secular robe of office had to supplant
the sacred one, and society had to separate itself into secular
hierarchies with secular uniforms and invest these with the
authority of as creed. And because, when the secular exalts
itself as the absolute, the result is always romanticism, so the
real and characteristic romanticism of that age was the cult
of the uniform, which implied, as it were, a superterrestrial
and supertemporal idea of uniform, an idea which did not
really exist and yet was so powerful that it took hold of men
far more completely than any secular vocation could, a non-
existent and yet so potent idea that it transformed the man
in uniform into a property of his uniform, and never into a
professional man in the civilian sense; and this perhaps simply
because the man who wears the uniform is content to feel
that he is fulfilling the most essential function of his age and
therefore guaranteeing the security of his own life.

The character Bertrand, note, does not present the idea of the
power of the uniform—Hermann Broch does, and it marks an
important difference. As it happens, a uniform, specifically the
military uniform, does play a significant role in the first volume
of *The Sleepwalkers*. Interesting, even brilliant, as this passage
is, Broch is remiss in not having found a way to have one of the
characters in his novel formulate the idea set out here instead
of presented by the author himself. The novel of ideas, in so far
as it features ideas over actions, is perhaps itself a bad idea. Too

aggressively put forth, ideas in fiction can corrode and ultimately destroy the fiction.

Closer to our own time, the novels of Saul Bellow tend to be all ideas, little plot, a literary version of "all hat, no cattle." Bellow did many literary things well, and some things brilliantly. He could describe urban landscapes, as well as the oddities of the human face and body—I shall never forget the vastly overweight character in one of his novels whose trousers seem to have had a "four-foot fly." But Bellow's powers of invention were slight. Most of the narrators of his novels were all too clearly Bellow surrogates or alter egos. These narrators expostulate, opinionate, ruminate about the fall of the West while wondering why them, why were they chosen to be so tortured by modernity? "To invent a new impersonator of Job is more or less his formula for getting a new book started," Hugh Kenner wrote of Saul Bellow, "someone whose 'Why me?' can extend to 'Why anyone?'"

Bellow's larger problem was his inability to create plots. From *TheAdventures of Augie March* on to *Ravelstein*, his novels tend to peter out, his endings rarely satisfy, and so finally the books themselves, though endowed with considerable charm as one reads along in them, finally seem neither memorable nor re-readable. Bellow was writing the novel of ideas but doing so through putting his ideas in the head and mouth of his Bellow-like narrators, his literary surrogates. He could make the ideas seem interesting, sometimes comic, occasionally (as in his novel *Herzog*) farcical, even dazzling, but without the propulsive power of plot they remain ideas chiefly. In his day Saul Bellow won all the prizes and was everywhere acclaimed, but he ended a less than fully successful novelist, his books more soliloquies than novels. If one were asked to summarize Bellow's *oeuvre* in fewer than ten words, the following might not be too far off: "An intellectual complains about the life of his times." Reading a Saul Bellow novel might be likened

to attending a concert of Yehudi Menuhin playing Mozart; one is
so intent on Menuhin's virtuosity that Mozart gets lost.

In the realm of intellectual sophistication, next to Saul Bellow,
Theodore Dreiser wasn't even a yokel. Such ideas as Dreiser had
were wretched. He fell for communism and fascism both. He was
not free of anti-Semitism. His lechery was such that you would
have been foolish to leave your great-grandmother alone in a room
with him. He was uneducated, untouched by culture. The ninth
of ten children, Dreiser was born to a German immigrant father
who never got a secure foothold in America and retreated into
extreme superstitious religiosity. The family moved often from one
small Indiana town to another, at one point living in a fire house
that was said also to serve as a brothel. His mother took in other
people's washing. His sisters cavorted with married men; his brothers lapsed into flashy living and alcoholism. Gawky and awkward,
he had buck teeth and an eye that wandered. Shame was part of
Dreiser's heritage.

One of the mysteries of art is itself highlighted by the career
of Theodore Dreiser, a man who in his personal life was a crank
and a bore, who believed that Franklin Delano Roosevelt was part
Jewish, and who wrote some of the most wretched sentences in all
of American literature. H. L. Mencken, who admired and cham-
pioned Dreiser's novels, said that he had "an incurable antipathy
for *le mot juste*," adding that "Every reader of the Dreiser novels
must cherish astounding specimens—of awkward, platitudinous
marginalia, of whole scenes spoiled by bad writing, of phrases as
brackish as so many lumps of sodium hyposulphite." Who but
Dreiser could write, "'Nothing doing,' he exclaimed in the slang of
the day." Or: "'Aw, you hush up,' was her displeased rejoinder." Or:
"The death house of this particular prison was one of those crass
erections and maintenances of human insensibility and stupidity for which no one was primarily responsible." Given Theodore

Dreiser's many shortcomings, how might one explain the enduring power of such novels of his as *Sister Carrie, Jennie Gerhardt,* and *An American Tragedy,* and of great stretches of *The Financier* and *The Titan*—novels written more than a century ago and still readable today?¶

IX.

THE ACHIEVEMENT of Theodore Dreiser is indirectly a comment on the limitation of style in fiction. Style has its pleasures, and these are not inconsiderable, but it is not, cannot be, the central attribute of great novelists. Those novelists who rely on style, along with those who rely on irony, aesthetically satisfying and entertaining though they can be, tend not to be among the most powerful, the truly great novelists.

How did it come about that Theodore Dreiser, clod and creep that he was, was able to write novels that not only told important truths about the way his countrymen lived but was able to do so in a powerful and persuasive way? (Saul Bellow, himself a stylish writer, puts the point well: "I often think the criticism of Dreiser as a stylist betrays a resistance to the feelings he causes readers to suffer. If they say he can't write, they need not experience those feelings.") Dreiser's great subject was the connection between individual character and destiny—a subject that has been at the heart of the work of such novelists as Stendhal, Balzac, George Eliot, Dickens, Tolstoy, Thomas Hardy, and Joseph Conrad. Owing to his own provincial and generally bleak background, Dreiser knew craving, fear, and humiliation at first hand; he knew the desolation that accompanies loneliness and the terror of failure in an uncaring universe—he knew all these things, and somehow he knew how to transfer them to the characters in his novels.

Theodore Dreiser could also write about less than fully sentient beings, as he for the most part did in *Sister Carrie* and *Jennie Gerhardt* and other of his novels. He understood better than writers much more sophisticated than he that we are all at the mercy of fate. He was properly impressed by the mystery of life. In "Life, Art and America," one of his rare essays, he wrote: "A man, if he can, should question the things that he sees—not some things, but everything—stand, as it were, in the middle of this whirling storm of contradiction which we know as life, and ask of it its sources and import." Owing to this questioning spirit, owing to his own longings, Dreiser could create such unforgettable characters as George Hurstwood, Jennie Gerhardt, Frank Cowperwood, and Clyde Griffiths. His subject as a novelist, as he once told an interviewer, was "life as it is, the facts as they exist, the game as it is played."

Dreiser was among those fast writers—Balzac, Dostoyevsky, and Solzhenitsyn among them—who wrote under financial or political strain, the urgency of which did not allow time for the niceties of style. I do not read Russian, but I'm told that the Russian of Dostoyevsky, who wrote under the pressure of gambling debts, can be very rough, and that over the years his translators have often needed to clean up his prose. Solzhenitsyn wrote his powerful early novels in a Siberian gulag, on paper that he needed to hide from authorities. (In the Soviet Union they took literature seriously—seriously enough to kill writers for going against Communist Party orthodoxy.) Balzac, a man greatly mistaken in his assessment of his own business acumen, wrote literally to keep creditors of his many poor investments from his door. Style in all these instances had to be forgone. Yet, somehow, it didn't, still doesn't, matter, not if a questing spirit and a large heart were at work.

I first read the great Russian novelists in college in the Penguin translations of Constance Garnett. I thought the novels then, as I think them now, marvelous, *nonpareil*. (I shouldn't like to have to choose between Tolstoy or Shakespeare as the greatest of all writers in the West, though I have long been impressed by Justice Holmes remarking of Shakespeare that whenever he reads him he is "struck by the reflection how a few golden sentences will float a lot of quibble and drool for centuries . . .") Only slightly later did I hear complaints about the quality of the Constance Garnett translations. Even in what might be thought an inadequate translation— and, without any Russian I am in no position to say that Mrs. Garnett's were that—the greatness of the great Russian novelists came through, which makes me wonder if one definition of a great novelist is that his or her power is apparent even in a poor translation. Other novelists, good as they are, seem untranslatable—for example, the late novels of Henry James.

As for those novelists known for their style, or stylishness, I think immediately of three: James Joyce, Vladimir Nabokov, and John Updike. All for me come under the category of novelists I admire without being particularly nuts about them. Joyce was of course a great innovator, devising the stream of consciousness and setting his novel *Ulysses* along lines parallel to Homer's *Odyssey*, all set out on the streets of Dublin in a single day: June 16, 1904—so-called Bloomsday, after the novel's protagonist, Leopold Bloom. I recently reread *Ulysses* and once again found myself much impressed but less than enamored of it. Even after recognizing Joyce's technical achievement, the novel's story, its characters, somehow, don't much move me. I find a soullessness to the proceedings. As for that Joycean exercise in elaborate and lengthy obscurity called *Finnegans Wake*, I have long enjoyed the anecdote about the literary critic who was sent a book with the title *A Key to Finnegans Wake*, and returned it with a note saying, "What *Finnegans Wake* needs is not a key but a lock."

Vladimir Nabokov was one of the grand masters of English—a statement all the more impressive when one considers English may have been his third, possibly his fourth language. He wrote no bad sentences, and endless elegant and amusing ones. But with few exceptions—such as a book many might consider minor among his works, the novel *Pnin*, along with a few of his short stories—there is a coldness in Nabokov's fiction. *Lolita*, his most famous work, a novel of pedophilia, I consider perhaps the most overrated work of the past century, a book of real interest only when Nabokov departs his main characters and does amusing descriptions of American life on the road. I like to think I know how good a writer Vladimir Nabokov was while also believing that the absence of largeness of heart kept him from becoming a truly great one.

John Updike produced no fewer than thirty-five books, among them works of poetry, essays, criticism, short-stories, and of course novels. Updike appears to have been serious in his Protestantism, and he never ran with the herd in his politics. He was not, for example, against the Vietnam War. I have not read anywhere near all he wrote, but those of his novels and short stories I have read tend to disappoint. The reason is partly the heavy doses of sex in his fiction—*Couples*, one of his most famous novels, might carry the subtitle, *Bonking Among the Suburban Middle Class*—but also his weakness for "fine" writing. Consider the Updike story "My Father's Tears," in which the main character recalls a rainbow that played on the bathroom walls of his first wife's family's house, where she had become pregnant: "This microscopic event deep within my bride became allied in my mind with the little rainbow low on the bathroom wall, our pet imp of refraction." This, I gather, is what is known as an epiphany, and though it seems to please Updike's character, I'll be damned if I as a reader know what to do with it. These bits pop up with some regularity in Updike stories. In much of his fiction Updike reached out to a wider world, especially in his four novels centered around the character of Harry Rabbit, high-school basketball star later turned Toyota dealer. Yet even in these novels one feels something missing, an element of gravity perhaps, a sense that the style employed is more significant than the content. One might say about John Updike what Arnold Bennett said of himself: "My work will never be better than third-rate, judged by the high standards, but I shall be cunning enough to make it impose on my contemporaries." ¶

X.

FICTION, AS HAS BEEN SAID, is a house of many mansions.
(Also a few modest bungalows, Quonset huts, and shanties.)
To pick up the housing metaphor, Ford Madox Ford, author of
Parade's End and *The Good Soldier* (which Robert Lowell called the
"best French novel in the English language"), noted how when lost
in a splendid novel, one feels one is living in a splendid house of
the novelist's creation:

> In such masterpieces of their genre as *Buddenbrooks* and *The
> Magic Mountain*, as with *Pride and Prejudice* or *Mansfield Park*,
> the personality of the author, projecting itself through the
> human instances he selects to render, gives one a pleasure that,
> seizing upon one with the first words one reads, continues to the
> last page. In that pleasure one omits to notice either the writer's
> methods or his social or political tendencies, and his books
> become, as it were, countrysides or manor houses rather than
> bound leaves of paper impressed with printed characters.

The occupant of one of these mansions, a substantial one,
a man so different from Theodore Dreiser as to seem almost to
belong to a different species, was Marcel Proust. Half-Jewish and
fully homosexual, in *In Search of Lost Time* Proust wrote a work
of roughly a million and quarter words, covering more than 3,200

pages in seven volumes. His novel is a mountain that many determined literary people have felt unable to climb. For those who
have climbed it, the view is dazzling. The novel is a study of life in
France's *belle époque* that in its anatomy of snobbery, its investigation of human motive, its psychological penetration generally, is
without peer.

The difference in sensibility and literary method between
Theodore Dreiser and Marcel Proust illustrates in boldface how
vast and various is the genre called the novel. So vast and various
is it that no poetics of the novel, such as that which Aristotle wrote
for the epic and the drama, has or can ever be written. The novel
comprises plot, action, character, thought, often moral theme;
it uses scene, summary, description, dialogue; point of view is
essential to it. Joseph Conrad, one of the most thoughtful of its
practitioners, wrote that the novel "must strenuously aspire to
the plasticity of sculpture, the color of painting, and to the magic
suggestiveness of music—which is the art of arts." Above all, of
course, it must produce the successful illusion of reality. Of his
own fiction, Conrad wrote: "My task, which I am trying to achieve
is, by the power of the written word, to make you hear, to make
you feel—it is, before all, to make you see. That—and no more, and
it is everything."

In *The Rise of the Novel*, Ian Watt writes that the central problem of the novel is "how to impose a coherent moral structure on
narrative without detracting from its air of literary authenticity."
The novel has had its share of not always fully clear "isms" ("natu-
ralism," "realism," "symbolism"), but the best novels elude all isms
and are centered on moral conflict. Sometimes this conflict is
between the public and private lives of its characters, sometimes
between desire and righteousness, sometimes between duty and
freedom. The possibilities and permutations are endless, which has
given the novel its incontestable richness. Novels have been written
without this moral component, but they are usually in the realm

of what has been termed the Literature of Escape, or works written for the simple pleasure of story, varying in quality from *The Three Musketeers* to *Fifty Shades of Grey*. Causality in the novel is rarely more interesting than when it is about morality. "Fiction," wrote Ford Madox Ford, ". . . had to pay an always greater tribute to morality as it escaped from being the mere servant of established religion." Religion, for those with faith, remains the great instructor and arbiter of morality. But the novel deals with morality on a more subtle level: it deals with the morality of specific actions and thoughts in a wide range of particulars. Jaroslav Hašek's *Good Soldier Švejk*, Joseph Roth's *The Radetzky March*, and Ford Madox Ford's *Parade's End* are three novels with military titles, all splendid and none in the least like the other. Every good novel is unlike every other good novel.

What the novel does better than any other form is allow its readers to investigate the inner, or secret, life of its characters. Often this life is not entirely known to the characters themselves, but it is known to the novelist, or had better be if the novel is to succeed. Nor is it going too far to say that we often come to know characters in novels better than we do friends or even family. The novel is the genre of intimacy. The closest possible view of the widest possible cast of characters, such does the novel provide, and in the hands of its masters it provides it *in excelsis*.

How did this extraordinary form, the novel, come into being? The form was with some few exceptions largely unknown to those two richest of classical cultures, the Greek and the Roman, though had the novel existed, Herodotus, Xenophon, and Plutarch might in their day have been major novelists. The novel was preceded, of course, by the epic, the lyric, and the staged drama, all forms that could survive without the aid of the printing press. Too lengthy for oral recitation, the novel needed the crucial advance in technology that was the development of widespread, or mass, printing from the sixteenth century on. Leisure was also required to read

the hefty tomes—*Don Quixote, Pamela, Clarissa, Tom Jones*—that
the early novelists tended to produce, and so novels may be said
to have awaited a rising middle class with the time to read them.
Increased urbanization and the rise of individualism were also key
components required for the advance of the novel.

Ian Watt's *Rise of the Novel* is the best account I know of the
early history of the novel, and much of what follows I have taken
from his pages. Toward the close of the eighteenth century, the
best estimate of the size of the reading public in England, a country then with a population of six million, was eighty thousand.
Nothing like a regular school system existed, and illiteracy was
more common than not. Mere subsistence among laborers was all-
encompassing, and the time for reading, even if one had the ability
to do so, was minimal.

Between 1700 and 1900, a grand age for the novel, literacy
in England rose to roughly 95 percent of the country. Between
1792 and 1802 English presses turned out some 372 books, the
majority of these religious books. How many of these 372 were
novels is not known, but all books in that day were expensive.
Only the prosperous middle class and above could afford to own
them, and among this privileged grouping chiefly women had
the leisure to read them. Lady Mary Wortley Montague was an
avid reader of novels, and so was Samuel Johnson's friend Hester
Thrale. Household servants may also have had the leisure to read,
and the books of their employers were, one gathers, often available to them. Pamela, in Samuel Richardson's novel of that name,
was herself a house maid.

The printer during these years was often also a bookseller. In
previous centuries, authors relied on the patronage of the nobility, a patronage that could often be disappointing. (Recall Samuel
Johnson's famous letter to his less-than-helpful patron Lord
Chesterfield in which he wrote: "Is not a Patron one who looks
with unconcern on a man struggling for life in the water, and,

when he has reached ground, encumbers him with help?") From
the end of the eighteenth century on, authors were in effect in
the market, competing with other authors for readers and pay-
ment. Some, Henry Fielding among them, felt that this would
both degrade authorship and lower the standard of literature. Yet,
as Ian Watt writes, "the most obvious result of the application of
primarily economic criteria to the production of literature was
to favour prose as against verse." Watt adds that the advent of
the author into the bookseller market "both assisted the development of one of the characteristic technical innovations of the
new form—its copious particularity of description and explanation—and made possible the remarkable independence of [such
novelists as] Defoe and Richardson from the classical critical
tradition which was an indispensable condition of their literary
achievement."

Specificity is of course at the heart of the novel. The novel deals
with individuals, the specific details of their lives, and in a way that
marked a distinct departure from the classical literary treatment
exhibited by Homeric heroes, Sophoclean tragic figures, Dantesque
types. The novel spread wider in its interests, and went deeper
in its details, than any earlier form of literature. In James Joyce's
Ulysses, Stephen Dedalus notes that "the supreme question about a
work of art is out of how deep a life does it spring." One criterion
for the success of a novel is how deeply does it go into the lives it
sets out to describe.

The novel's concentration on the individual was at the time of
its efflorescence in the early eighteenth century coterminous with a
similar concentration on individual lives in English society generally. Ian Watt writes: "The novel's serious concern with the daily
lives of ordinary people seems to depend upon two important
general conditions: the society must value every individual highly
enough to consider him the proper subject of its serious literature; and there must be enough variety of belief and action among

ordinary people for a detailed account of them to be of interest to other ordinary people, the readers of novels."

Industrialization via capitalism and the rise of modern Protestantism, both widening the possibilities for freedom of action, further advanced the prospects for the novel. The heroes of novels were no longer exclusively or even chiefly aristocrats but men and women attempting to survive and distinguish themselves under the new economic order. The first, now classic case, of course, was Daniel Defoe's Robinson Crusoe, a man who, shored up alone on an island, had to make his own economy. Since Descartes' "I think, therefore I am," philosophers tended to favor the particular; and the particular, or specific cases of ordinary people, is what the novel is, and always has been, about.

Some novelists dwell on the everydayness of life, slowly demonstrating what matters most in their characters' lives; others feature dramatic events, life changing *peripeteias*, or reversals of fortune, after which nothing is the same. Tolstoy is a notable example of the former kind of novelist, Dostoyevsky of the latter. In some novels actual historical figures appear, as Napoleon does in *War and Peace* and Joseph Stalin does in Solzhenitsyn's *August 1914*. But apart from so-called "historical novels," they do not dominate. Henry James defined the novel as "a representation of life," and the lives represented are always more or less sapient but generally identifiably ordinary people. Along the way, through such representation, better novels will, in a manner more or less subtle, touch on the vagaries of fate and enlarge on our sense of human nature. Destiny is the supra-theme of every powerful novel.

The divide between those who read novels as a form of escape from the dullness of quotidian life and those who read them seeking aesthetic pleasure and intellectual discovery can of course be considerable. In her *Fiction and the Reading Public* (1939), Q. D. Leavis writes that people read novels for four general reasons: "1) To pass time not unpleasantly. 2) To obtain vicarious satisfaction or compensation for life. 3) To obtain assistance in the business of living. 4) To enrich the quality of living by extending, deepening, refining, co-ordinating experience." Sometimes these reasons combine; few readers go to novels for all four reasons; and implicit in the four reasons is a division between high and low culture. Only a sophisticated reader, for example, would read novels for reason number four, but that doesn't preclude that same reader from turning to novels for reason number one.

The sub-theme of Q. D. Leavis's book is the diminishment of highculture over the past three or so centuries and the effect this has had on the production and quality of novels. In her reading of cultural history, people of an earlier time, less distracted by journalism, cinema, and television—she wrote before the onset of the Internet, perhaps the greatest distraction of all—were able to find deeper pleasure in novels than we do in the modern era.

Mrs. Leavis holds that the novel, at its best, can "help the reader to deal less inadequately with [life]; the novel can deepen, extend, and refine experience by allowing the reader to live at the expense of an unusually intelligent and sensitive mind, by giving him access to a finer code than his own." More and more, she believed, modern novels failed to do this, and instead actually got "in the way of genuine feeling and responsible thinking by creating cheap mechanical responses and by throwing weight on the side of social, national, and herd prejudices"

Q. D. Leavis posits a prelapsarian time, before the rise of industrialism turned peasants into proletarians, when, she contends, music "filled the leisure of the rich and poor and the working hours of the people as well." She harks back to an era when "the governing class was cultivated." Nearly every household had copies of the King James Bible and John Bunyan's *Pilgrim's Progress*. Those who were able to read had the patience to disentangle the complex prose of Thomas Browne and Richard Burton. This was an age, fortunate in her view, without "any distractions

of the kind that beset the twentieth century." The turning point
for her was the nineteenth century. "The difference between the
popular novels of the eighteenth century and of the nineteenth,"
she writes, "is that the new fiction instead of requiring its readers to co-operate in a sophisticated entertainment discovers 'the
great heart of the public.'"

Charles Dickens, for whose writing Mrs. Leavis, like her
husband F. R Leavis, has little regard, "stands primarily for a set of
crude emotional exercises. He discovered, for instance, the formula 'laughter and tears' that has been the foundation of practi-
cally every popular success ever since (Hollywood's as well as the
bestseller's).... These are the tears that rise in the heart and gather
to the eyes involuntarily or even in spite of the reader, though an
alert critical mind may cut them off at the source in a revulsion to
disgust." ("One must have a heart of stone not to laugh at the death
of Little Nell," wrote Oscar Wilde of that famous scene in Dickens's
The Old Curiosity Shop.)

The cheapening of entertainment has radically altered even
the patience of the modern man or woman, according to Mrs.
Leavis, so that "it is only the exceptional character that can toler-
ate solitude and silence, distressing to modern nerves." Part of this
cheapening afflicted the novel itself, she argues, and so the habit
kicked in of reading poor novels, not so much to pass time, but, as
Samuel Taylor Coleridge had it, to "kill time."

D. H. Lawrence felt that the problem began when philosophy
and fiction, such as is displayed in Plato's *Dialogues*, parted com-
pany. In his essay "The Future of the Novel," Lawrence writes: "It
seems to me it was the greatest pity in the world, when philosophy and fiction got split. They used to be one, right from the dark
days of myth. Then they went and parted, like a nagging married
couple, with Aristotle and Thomas Aquinas and that beastly Kant.
So the novel went sloppy, and philosophy went abstract-dry. The
two should come together again, in the novel." But is this really the
chief problem of the novel?

A hard woman, the late Q. D. Leavis, but not an unintelligent one. Yet one distrusts the prelapsarian time she depicts, when men and women were more centered and impervious to all but superior culture. All paradises, as Proust reminds us, are lost paradises, which is to say that most probably never really existed. My own sense, based on thirty years of university teaching, is that at all times only a small, really a quite minuscule number of people are truly passionate about culture and intent on reaping its rewards. What impresses, though, is how intensely that minuscule number comes to value culture. A few people among them are born into homes where high culture is on offer, but, in my experience, most are not. Instead they come upon it almost by accident. Most artists—visual, musical, literary—turn out not to be from the upper- but from the middle- and lower-middle classes.

Mrs. Leavis also overlooks that often people come to the higher culture she much admires up from the ladder that begins with lower culture. Along with Mrs. Leavis, the critic Dwight Macdonald in his day based much of his career on (to him) the necessary separations among high-, middle-, and low-brow culture. But those separations, and the distinctions implicit in them, can also sometimes seem unrealistic, if not hollow. Reading less-than-great novels when young can give one a taste for fiction that slowly grows more subtle and demanding. Many who are otherwise authentically highbrow in their intellectual and aesthetic tastes retain an interest in less-than-highbrow reading. (Two highly intelligent acquaintances of mine, Irving Kristol and the historian Eugen Weber, had a passionate interest in detective fiction, as did W. H. Auden and Jacques Barzun.) Critics like Macdonald used to mock the Book of the Month Club, which selected books, many of them novels, for its members, as irredeemably middle-brow. (Two of the Book of the Month Club's "main selections," it needs to be remembered, were Richard Wright's *Native Son* and George Santayana's *The Last Puritan*.) Culture can be a ladder, up which many of us, given the conditions in which we were born, climb; nor do we always remain on the same rung.

Brought up by intelligent parents whose lives were otherwise too crowded to allow much time for any reading beyond newspapers and a few popular magazines, I went off to the University of Illinois with little more in mind than coming out four years later as that then-vaunted personage, a college graduate. Much of the education I encountered at Illinois chiefly entailed memorization: of biological phyla, of irregular French verbs, of six reasons for the Renaissance and nine for the French Revolution. None of this felt much like education to me.

At the University of Chicago, to which I transferred after my freshman year, the cultural stakes were raised considerably. There I read Freud and Marx and Tocqueville and Max Weber and lots of Plato and Aristotle. I took two different courses in the novel: one a survey from *The Princess of Cleves* to *Ulysses*, the other devoted to such modern novelists as E. M. Forster, Hemingway, Faulkner, Ford Madox Ford, and Evelyn Waugh, among others. I read all these novels with the limited comprehension of a twenty-year-old, but I sensed, somehow, that something significant, if still beyond my full understanding, was going on in their pages.

Teaching novels, unlike teaching poetry and drama and much history, is unsatisfactory, or so at least I felt over the years in my own teaching of the novels of Henry James, Joseph Conrad, Thomas Mann, Theodore Dreiser, Willa Cather, and others. One could explain that in *In Search of Lost Time* Proust employed a Bergsonian sense of time. But having done that, what has one really done, except implicitly suggest that perhaps one did better to cut out Proust and read Henri Bergson directly? This was the last thing I should ever want to do. Suggesting influence, one could say that in his novel Proust combines and incorporates the best of his French predecessors Balzac and Stendhal, but having said that one hasn't, really, said all that much. One could demonstrate the correspondences of James Joyce's *Ulysses* to Homer's *Odyssey*, but here one hasn't done all that much either. Something larger, something grander, is going on in great novels than their use of the ideas or the influence upon them of other writers and writings.¶

XI.

HOW DOES ONE JUDGE A NOVEL? Not, perhaps the first
thing to say is, easily. A novel is less readily graspable than a poem
or play; it is not subject to the same standards of accuracy as history or biography, though it can of course be judged preposterous if
its characters or twists in its plot are unconvincing. The difference
between biography and the novel is noteworthy. Biographies provide both pleasure and instruction. The best of biographies, from
James Boswell's *Life of Samuel Johnson* to Richard Ellmann's *James
Joyce* to Leon Edel's five-volume *Henry James*, can take us deep
into the lives of their subjects, yet only so deep. They can tell us
what the public thought of their subjects, what their closest friends
and family thought of them, and sometimes (if candid diaries and
crucial letters are available) what they thought of themselves. But
biographers cannot, as the best novelists can, tell us about their
secret desires, their deepest disappointments, their most ardent
longings—they cannot tell us, as novelists who know their characters as well as themselves can, about matters of the heart.

   The Russian critic Mikhail Bakhtin wrote that no individual
can be "completely incarnated into the flesh of existing socio-his-
torical categories." The reason is that is "no mere form that would
be able to incarnate once and forever all of his human possibilities and needs, no form in which he could exhaust himself down
to the last word.... There always remains an unrealized surplus of

humaneness." That surplus entails the changeability, the unpredict-
ability, the unending variousness of human thought and behavior.
Novels can run from fifty thousand or so words to Proust's 1.25
million words. Some, like drowning sailors, cling to the surface of
their story; others dive down to the lowest depths of the psyche.
Novelists tell stories, set scenes, describe actions, provide dialogue,
organize plots. Some novelists do one or another of these things
extremely well; others do some of them better than others. A rare
few do them all excellently. One can describe a novel, but short of
retelling it, word for word, one cannot hope to grasp it all, either
for recounting to others or even to oneself. What a novel can do,
by presenting a life or lives different from, sometimes foreign to,
one's own, is expand one's sympathies (sometimes), alter one's taste
(often), widen the lenses of one's own experience (always), and
take one outside of oneself (if one is lucky).

One should read a novel with sympathetic attention, obviously.
Barriers to this sympathy might be a novelist's rebarbative style
(many people claim this kills the novels of Theodore Dreiser for
them), his objectionable point of view (Louis-Ferdinand Céline's
anti-Semitism qualifies nicely here), or his politics (unless one
shares E. L. Doctorow's relentless anti-Americanism, one is likely
to find his novels hard going). But even in novelists one finds
objectionable, it is possible to find good things. In his essay *The
Fine Art of Reading*, Lord David Cecil writes that "genius—the dis-
tinguishing quality of the individual genius, that is what matters,"
and goes on to note: "There are as many different kinds of good
books as there are different kinds of good writer. Each has something to give us. We should admire each in so far as he strikes us as
good in his particular kind."

Taste of course enters in. "There is no accounting for or disput-
ing taste," or so runs a platitude of long standing. Yet one can in
fact account for good taste, which one acquires partly by instinct
and temperament but chiefly by training and experience. One's

taste is trained by wide reading, listening to lots of elevated music, viewing a great many of the best paintings and sculptures. As for temperament, it is temperament combined with taste that makes one prefer Jane Austen over Ernest Hemingway, Marcel Proust over Gustave Flaubert, Evelyn Waugh over Donald Barthelme, Willa Cather over Mary McCarthy.

Taste in reading develops in circuitous, not to say often strange ways. The metaphor of a ladder of taste in fiction, running from the low rungs of Stephen King, James Patterson, and E. L. James to the high rungs of Henry James, Marcel Proust, and Virginia Woolf, a metaphor I used earlier, isn't quite accurate. As there is no true progress in the arts—no age in music, for example, has ever come near touching that which produced Bach, Beethoven, Mozart, and Haydn, or none in the visual arts that compares with that of the Renaissance—so in the history of the novel there are only greater and lesser periods. Is Virginia Woolf a greater novelist than George Eliot, James Joyce greater than Leo Tolstoy? I don't believe so. The development of taste in reading novels is finally about the advancement of one's appetite for the richness of human experience. At a certain point in one's reading life, James Michener's *Hawaii*, Ayn Rand's *Fountainhead*, James Jones's *From Here to Eternity* satisfy that appetite. But a true literary gourmand soon demands richer fare. ¶

XII.

TIME TAKES ITS TOLL on novels. Some novels are imprisoned in their day, and hence nearly inaccessible to readers of a later day. George Eliot was in many ways—in her morality, in her general outlook—a Victorian, but she also happened to be a genius, which allowed her to transcend her Victorianism. *Don Quixote*, written in two parts in 1605 and 1615 and running to more than nine hundred pages, is still readable, and so are most of the nineteenth-century Russians—Gogol, Tolstoy, Dostoyevsky, Goncharov, Leskov—the best of the Victorian novelists, and the novels of Joseph Roth, Tomasi di Lampedusa, the Brothers Singer (I. B., and I. J.), and yet still others.

What qualities make a novel live long after its composition? Can one judge which novels among contemporaries or near contemporaries are likely to pass the crucial, the ultimate literary test of longevity? I have myself been asked who among novelists of my lifetime are likely to be read—to be still readable—a half century or more from now. The only answer I supply with any confidence is Isaac Bashevis Singer. He was a genuine storyteller, a man who made you ardently want to know what happens next. In the stories he told one always feels a great deal more is at stake than mere storytelling alone. Whether living in eighteenth-century Poland or twentieth-century Manhattan, his characters are put to every ethical test, made to face all temptations. A universality emerges

out of their very specificity, a strong sense of timelessness even
though they are firmly anchored in a unique period and place.
Singer's characters are seekers, looking for deeper meaning in life,
known to argue even with God. Singer knew what so many writers
younger than he seem to have forgot, that imagination alone is not
enough; it is the moral imagination, carefully calibrating the meaning of human acts, that makes for great fiction.

At the same time the novels of Norman Mailer, Philip Roth,
and John Updike, so popular and widely written about in their day,
have already begun to lose interest. Mailer, Roth, Updike, and other of the novelists of the past fifty or so years who wrote so heavily
about sex, setting it out in their novels in an elaborately detailed
way, making it absolutely central to character and plot, already
begin to seem of much diminished interest, their novels difficult
to read because of what now seems an adolescent emphasis on sex.
These novelists, living in the shadow of a coarse Freudianism, writing in an age before the widespread use of the pill, when so much
was riding on sex for women (fear of pregnancy, concern about
reputation), taking sex as the motor force of human behavior, often
placed sex as the central drama of their novels.

Imagine if Mailer, Roth, & Co. wrote any of the great novels of
the past. If Norman Mailer had written James's *Portrait of a Lady*,
Gilbert Osmond would doubtless have required fellatio of Isabelle
Archer. If John Updike had written George Eliot's *Middlemarch*,
Edward Casaubon might well have suffered *ejaculatio praecox*. If
Alan Hollinghurst, the gay English novelist, had been the author
of Willa Cather's *Death Comes for the Archbishop*, one of the two
priests in that novel would likely have put homosexual moves
on the other. Don't ask what Count Aleksey Vronsky would have
requested of Anna if Philip Roth had written *Anna Karenina*.
With sex details added, four great novels would have gone down
the tubes.

Because of the emphasis on sex in his novels, if he is to be remembered at all, Norman Mailer is likely to be remembered for a tedious story called "The Time of Her Time" about a woman's having her first orgasm. Likewise Philip Roth for *Portnoy's Complaint*, his book about masturbation whose most memorable passage is "So. Now you know the worst I have ever done. I fucked my own family's dinner"; as well as John Updike for the unhappy phrase "cunty fingers."

The *Literary Review* has for more than twenty-five years now offered its Bad Sex in Fiction Award, honoring the wretched descriptions of sex written by such novelists as Mailer, Nancy Huston, Tom Wolfe, and others. Here, from the 2005 winner, a novelist named Giles Coren, is a fairly mild sampler: "We made our way to the summerhouse and hid in its shadows. We lay on the cool floor and I twined my legs around Homer's body, gripping him like a hunter hanging on to its prey. He made love to me with his fingers and I came in the palm of his hand. He stroked my breasts and neck. 'Don't wash it away,' he said. 'I want to be able to smell you tonight.'" Charming? The very reverse of charming—creepy, I should say. From among the other Bad Sex in Fiction Award winners much worse could be quoted.

In my own stories, plots do occasionally call for characters to wind up in bed together. A shy pornographer—or, as I prefer to think myself, a sly pornographer—I cannot put myself, let alone my readers, through the naming of (private) parts, and then the showing of those parts in action. Instead I have always thought it best to allow my readers to imagine rather than read what has gone on behind closed bedroom doors. In one such story of mine, called "The Count and the Princess," about the love between a Polish émigré and a middle-age Jewish housewife, I set the scene and then close the door:

> He bent over to pour the tea, but his hands shook. The tea pot made a great clatter against the thin China cup and saucer. Mrs.

Skolnik put her hand over his to steady it. He turned and her eyes were only inches from his. He stood, and so did she; her robe had come slightly open. He was about to speak, when she gently covered his mouth with her hand. They embraced and she took him by the hand into the bedroom, where they did things together that the Count hadn't even dared to dream.

In another story called "Kizerman and Feigenbaum," my narrator winds up in the bed of an attractive women named Dinky Shapiro, a woman he knew in high school who was then out of reach because of her greater status, and about whom he could only fantasize. He, the narrator of the story, notes: "I'm not going to attempt to describe what Dinky and I did in her bed. I'm not that great at description. I'll only say that at the conclusion I didn't want my money back"

Yet again, from a story called "The Love Song of A. Jerome Minkoff":

Minkoff looked at his eyes in the rearview mirror. He had spent four extraordinary hours in a room upstairs in the airport Hilton with Mrs. Friedman—make that Larissa. After checking his male patients for testicular cancer, Minkoff always inquired, "Everything all right down there?" Who knew how many prescriptions in recent years he had written for Viagra, Cialis, Levitra, and the rest? He hadn't himself entirely neglected things down there, but Larissa Friedman had refreshed his memory of how revivifying they could be. She was a woman of experience. Although himself an easy A student in anatomy and the veteran of nearly forty years of medical practice, she was in possession of a few things about the physiology of the human body that until now had never occurred to Dr. A. Jerome Minkoff.

Do novels and stories really require sex, the physical activity, the bonking, planking, plonking, shagging, mating of beasts, and the scores of other names that physical love goes by? Is what people do in the bedroom all that revealing of human character, personality, even oddity? Isaac Bashevis Singer could be a sexy but was never a blatantly sexual writer; he recognized the force of sex without needing in his novels and stories to go into the intricate details. In an essay on the heavily sex-laden novels of a writer named Garth Greenwell, the novelist Sigrid Nunez writes:

> What I've always been highly unsure of, though, is how much a person's sex life defines who that person is, and how much it can really tell us—or even the person themselves [sic]—about the rest of their being. I will never be convinced, as some people apparently are, that we are most ourselves when we are in bed (indeed it seems to me that the number of people for whom this might be true must be quite small), or that all that much can be known about a person from the way they perform, or fail to perform, the sexual act, or by their individual erotic tastes. Maybe this is partly because I have never noticed big—if any—changes in the personalities of people I know during times when I happened to be aware they were having lots of sex and the times when I was aware they were having little or none. Nor have I seen significant differences, in other areas of their lives, between people I know who are wildly promiscuous and those who are celibate.

When writing about sex was legally prohibited, doing so seemed chancy, daring, brave even. Perhaps the most famous of banned books in the modern era was James Joyce's *Ulysses*. Quoting here from a Politics & Prose Bookshop note, the book was "the object of ire even before its full publication. *Ulysses* was burned in serialized form in the U.S. in 1918 before it was burned as a published manuscript in Ireland in 1922, Canada in 1922, and England in 1923. The book was officially banned in England in 1929, possibly because the mass-burning proved insufficient to

suppress its readership." The ban on the novel in the United States
was finally lifted in 1933, by Judge John Woolsey, of the United
States District Court for the Southern District of New York, whose
legal opinion ended: "I am quite aware that owing to some of its
scenes *Ulysses* is a rather strong draught to ask some sensitive
though normal person to take. But my considered opinion, after
long reflection, is that whilst in many places the effect of *Ulysses*
on the reader is somewhat emetic, nowhere does it tend to be an
aphrodisiac."

  In 1960, D. H. Lawrence's last novel, *Lady Chatterley's Lover*,
was prosecuted under England's Obscene Publications Act. An
impressive lineup of thirty-five witnesses—among them such
English writers as Rebecca West, E. M. Forster, and Richard
Hoggart—appeared at a hearing on the novel's behalf, attesting
to its literary quality, with the result that the novel was found not
obscene. Owing to the publicity of the trial, 200,000 copies of
the novel were said to have been sold the day after the ban on it
was lifted, leaving most of these readers to discover that, however
legally un-obscene the novel may have been, it also happens to be,
in the words of George Lyttelton, "an extremely dull and portent-
ously silly and pretentious book." Henry Miller's sex-ridden *Tropic
of Capricorn* and *Tropic of Cancer* novels were also long under the
lash of censorship and had to be brought out, in plain green covers,
by Maurice Girodias' quasi-outlaw Olympia Press in Paris, which
also published the first edition of Vladimir Nabokov's *Lolita*. As
a college student, I remember my excitement at obtaining one of
those green-covered paperback novels of Miller's—the excitement
of the illicit, which for the first hundred or so pages was sufficient
to block out how, in Truman Capote's phrase, "balls-achingly bor-
ing" the book was.

  These earlier literary trials doubtless lent an aura of path-
breaking to writing openly and in a detailed way about sex. In his
first, best-selling novel, *The Naked and The Dead* (1948), Norman

Mailer not only refrained from writing about sex but felt he had
to have his wartime soldiers forego the F-bomb—or what Clifton
Fadiman, in an amusing phrase, called "the coital intensifier"—
in favor of the word "fug." He would later excruciatingly detail
heterosexual sodomy in his historical novel about Egypt, *Ancient
Evenings*. Philip Roth's and John Updike's early books were, so to
say, bonkless, and better for it.

Women novelists soon got into the sex act. Erica Jong wrote
Fear of Flying, an international best-seller about what she called the
"zipless fuck," or fantasy of perfect sex, featuring such sentences as:
"And at that moment, I fell madly in love with him. His limp prick
had penetrated where a stiff one would never have reached." The
English novelist Brigid Brophy, in her novel *The Snow Ball*, provided a view of female orgasm: "suffering, sobbing, swelling, sawing,
sweating, her body was at last convulsed by the wave that broke
inside it." All that is missing here is the query, "And how about you,
Sweetie, how was it for you?"

The best single thought about sex, the act itself, that I know
came from my friend Hilton Kramer, who in conversation once
remarked that "all sex is comic, except one's own." (For a literary
treatment of sex as essentially comic, an example is E. M. Schorb's
2019 novel *R&R*.) Apart from comic treatment, though, the novelist does best to leave the detailed treatment of sex to the dirty-jokes
department and instead treat it for what it really is and as subse-
quent generations have come to view it: a (mostly indoor) sport
that at its best yields much pleasure.¶

XIII.

ISSUING OUT OF THE LIVES of the saints and the adventure romances of the crusades and the *Arabian Nights* and the stories of King Arthur's court, the novel over its history has taken many sub-forms: the *Bildungsroman*, the family chronicle, the novel of disillusionment, the *roman à clef*, and more. So many and various are the forms that a novel can take that the genre is perhaps best thought the formless form. But whatever else it may be, the novel is always about human existence, its delights and miseries, its triumphs and travails.

Despite its immensely impressive achievements, the announcement of the Death of The Novel has over the years become something close to a regular event. The funeral announcement for the novel is an old standby for the gloomy minded. Like the premature reports of Mark Twain's death, reports about the demise of the novel have often seemed "greatly exaggerated." Yet just now talk about the death of the novel has a credibility it has not quite had before.

Some saw the beginning of the end of the novel as far back as mid-nineteenth century. As early as 1856, in their *Journal*, the Goncourt brothers, writing of Edgar Allen Poe, who was much admired in France, noted that Poe was bringing on "a new literary world, pointing to a literature of the twentieth century. Scientific miracles, fables on the pattern A + B; a clear-sighted, sickly literature. No more poetry, but analytic fantasy. Something monomaniacal. Things playing a more important part than people; love giving way to deductions and other sources of ideas, style, subject, and interest; the basis of the novel transferred from the heart to the head, from the passion to the idea, from the drama to the denouement."

Fast forward a hundred and sixty years to find the contemporary English novelist Will Self asking in the May 2, 2014, English *Guardian*, "How do you think it feels to have dedicated your entire adult life to an art form only to see the bloody thing dying before your eyes?" Self continues: "In the early 1980s, and I would argue throughout the second half of the last century, the literary novel was perceived to be the prince of art forms, the cultural capstone and the apogee of creative endeavor. The capability words have when arranged sequentially to both mimic the free flow of human thought and investigate the physical expressions and interactions of thinking subjects; the way they may be shaped into a believable simulacrum of either the commonsensical world, or any number of invented ones; and the capability of the extended prose form itself, which, unlike any other art form, is able to enact self-analysis, to describe other aesthetic modes and even mimic them." But, according to Self, not any longer.

The sadness of this, Will Self argues, is that "there's still no substitute for the experience of close reading as we've come to understand and appreciate it—the capacity to imagine entire worlds from parsing a few lines of text; the ability to achieve deep and meditative levels of absorption in others' psyches" that only the novel offers. For Will Self, the short attention span that is one of the reigning side effects of digital culture is in good part responsible for the decline in the importance of the novel. He feels that even movies are in the grip of losing their interest for large segments of the population. "I believe the serious novel will continue to be written and read," he writes, "but it will be an art form on a par with easel painting or classical music: confined to a defined social and demographic group, requiring a degree of subsidy, a subject for historical scholarship rather than public discourse."

The great enemy for Will Self is that greatest of all mixed blessings, the Internet. The world has until now never known a distraction of its pervasiveness. When television became widespread, people talked about its destroying not only the movies but human concentration. But at least one couldn't carry one's television set around with one, the way one can carry the Internet, through the ownership of a cellphone or tablet, in one's pocket or purse. I write as if I am superior to the attractions of the Internet. Let me assure you, I am not. I do not go out without my cellphone, not even downstairs in the elevator to pick up the mail. I must check that phone for email no fewer than twenty times a day, though twenty-five might be closer to it, every day, including almost immediately after waking.

As for the Internet itself, I find its vast fund of information immensely useful. In the writing of this book, I do not know how many times I have called on Google or Wikipedia to check spellings or dates or quotations. I also find it useful as an *aide-memoire* to recall the names of actors, athletes, politicians, and much more that has slipped my mind. As someone who sends manuscripts off to editors and publishers, the speedy delivery of manuscripts and the quickness of return response is another gift of the Internet I much appreciate. Writing on a computer has made revision, where in my view writing really begins, vastly easier. In all these regards, and more besides, the Internet has been beneficial, a blessing really.

On the other, shakier hand, its powers of distraction may well be unfathomable. Since the advent of the cellphone, the tablet, and the laptop, in airports and on buses and trains, one less and less often sees people reading books or even newspapers. As soon as a plane lands, out come cellphones. I live in a neighborhood with two nearby retirement homes and a block or so away from a university. Gazing out at the street from my sixth- story apartment window, it sometimes seems as if the entire population of the neighborhood is bent over, the elderly over their walkers, the young over their cellphones, thumb-pumping away, emailing, googling, Wikipediaing, chat-rooming, face-timing, Redditting, porno-viewing, Lord knows what else. Since the invention of the automobile, surely no invention has changed the way people live as radically as has the Internet.

What I find most worrisome about the Internet is its capacity to change reading habits. One doesn't read on the Internet quite the same way one does on the printed page of a book or magazine or newspaper. The main reason one goes to the Internet to begin with is for information. One goes there, that is, chiefly to find out facts, and little more. Between information and knowledge there is a gap quite as large as that between knowledge and wisdom. If I discover, or someone sends me, an article or other item of more than three or so pages length on the Internet, I find I tend to read it with impatience, my hand on my mouse, itching to scroll down, to get, figuratively and literally both, to the bottom line. I rarely skim books or magazines. Online I rarely fail to skim items of any appreciable length.

The Internet, something about the very nature of the pixels in which its words and numbers appear, both encourages skimming and slights careful reading. Who, after all, would prefer to read a poem or a short story online rather than on page? Reading online, one tends to be less interested in all those details and small but important touches that make for interesting writing. While reading online any interest in well-made sentences, wit, interesting vocabulary, and all else that makes for superior writing tends to be scuppered. "Just the facts, Ma'am," as Sergeant Friday used to say on the old *Dragnet* television program. Just the facts and no nonsense about elegance, insight, and pleasing prose—the pursuit of facts is what the Internet is chiefly about. The Internet is made for, may in our day be the leading cause of, a national shortened attention span.

In *Proust and the Squid*, Maryanne Wolf sees the danger of the Internet as potentially going well beyond shortening the supply of readers for serious fiction. She asks: "Will unguided information [of the kind on offer in endless supply online] lead to an illusion of knowledge, and thus curtail the more difficult, time-consuming, critical thought processes that lead to knowledge itself? Will the split-second immediacy of information gained from a search engine and the sheer volume of what is available derail the slower, more deliberative processes that deepen our understanding of complex concepts, of another's inner thought processes, and of our own consciousness?" The answer to both questions, surely, is yes.

Maryanne Wolf goes on to write: "What would be lost to us if we replaced the skills honed by the reading brain with those now being formed in the new generation of 'digital natives,' who sit and read transfixed before a screen?" In *Proust and the Squid* she asks whether the new digital readers will lose the imagination needed to enter into the reading of novels, and wonders "whether typical young readers view the analysis of text and the search for deeper levels of meaning as more and more anachronistic because they are so accustomed to the immediacy and seeming comprehensiveness of the on-screen information—all of which is available without critical effort, and without any apparent need to go beyond the information provided. I ask, therefore, whether our children are learning the heart of the reading process: going beyond the text."

Something there is twitchy, nervous, hectic about all this thumb-pumping, googling, Siri- and Alexa-harkening that is at the heart of our digital culture. Something, more to the point, that seems the opposite of, if not outright opposed to, the calm and repose required by reading books, especially books of serious fiction. Something there is about reading on the Internet that is at base anti-literary.

Yet so strong is the pull of the Internet that it may well be that the true culture war of the future will not be between generations, or between people with implacably opposed political views, or between different races or ethnic groups or social classes, but between pixels and print for cultural supremacy. The English writer Kit Wilson has speculated that "maybe in a few hundred years' time, historians will look back at the advent of [Internet] forums at the start of the twenty-first century and see them not as a way for brain-fried, decadent millennial to pass time, but as the West's ingenious way of replacing the novel: the creation of entirely new arenas in which to explore our subjective experience." Wilson then adds: "Still, from the perspective of the present, you have to wonder if it is working: younger generations report that they are lonelier, and feel their lives are less meaningful, than ever. And in any case, the gulf between novel and forum appears vast: for one, online, we are encouraged only to seek out experiences that reflect, and thus validate, our own—we only ever really flesh out in our minds, therefore, the finer details of our own circumstances, not the depths of the human condition as a whole." That condition, of course, has long been the domain of the novel.

By now there are novels being published whose background and setting are the Internet itself, whose principal characters, finding their emotional lives online, are digitally addicted. I have not read any of these novels; life is too short, even for someone with the leisure to write a small book about the fate of the novel. But from reviews of these novels they sound immeasurably sad. In one such novel, a character's cellphone is stolen and "its loss leaves her feeling lighter." In another, when something a character puts online goes viral, "it blazed away the morning and the afternoon, it blazed like the new California, which we had come to accept as being always on fire. She ran back and forth in the flames, not eating or drinking, emitting a high-pitched sound most humans couldn't hear."

A recent *New Yorker* story, "Unread Messages" (July 12 & 19, 2021) by Sally Rooney, a portion of a novel in progress, has a leading character whose life is lived chiefly online. Here is a sample paragraph:

> After eating, she entered her bedroom. Through the window, the street below was visible, and the slow swell of the river. She removed her jacket and shoes, took the clasp from her hair, and drew her curtains shut. She took off her sweater and wriggled out of her trousers, leaving both items crumpled on the floor. Then she pulled on a cotton sweatshirt and a pair of gray leggings. Her hair, dark and falling loosely over her shoulders, looked clean and slightly dry. She climbed onto her bed and opened her laptop. For some time, she scrolled through various media timelines, occasionally opening and half reading long articles about elections overseas. Her face was wan and tired. Opening a private browser window on her laptop, the woman accessed a social-media Web site, and typed the words "aidan lavin" into the search box. A list of results appeared, and without glancing at the other options she clicked on the third result. A profile opened onscreen, displaying the name Aidan Lavin below a photograph of a man's head and shoulders viewed from behind. The man's hair was thick and dark and he was wearing a denim jacket. Beneath the photograph, a caption read: local sad boy. normal brain haver. check out the soundcloud. The user's most recent update, posted three hours earlier, was a photograph of a pigeon in a gutter, its head buried inside a discarded crisp packet. The caption read: same. The post had a hundred and twenty-seven likes. In her bedroom, leaning against the headboard of the unmade bed, the woman clicked on this post,

and replies appeared underneath. One reply, from a user with
the handle Actual Death Girl, read: looks like you and all. The
Aidan Lavin account had replied: youre right, insanely hand-
some. Actual Death Girl had liked this reply. The woman on her
laptop clicked through to the profile of the Actual Death Girl
account. After spending thirty-six minutes looking at a range of
social-media profiles associated with the Aidan Lavin account,
the woman shut her laptop and lay down on her bed.

Later the same woman, whose name we learn is Eileen, is
alone in bed at eleven o'clock, "curled up on her side, her makeup
smeared slightly under her eyes":

> Squinting at the screen of her phone, she tapped the icon of a
> social-media app. The interface opened and displayed a loading
> symbol. Eileen moved her thumb over the screen, waiting for it
> to load, and then suddenly closed the app. She navigated to her
> contacts, selected "Simon," and hit the call button. After three
> rings, he picked up and said, Hello?

As one can probably no longer write a detective story without
policemen searching out clues on their computers and pack-
ing their smartphones along with their guns, so the novels and
stories of the future may well, alas, require characters with apps
instead of traits, on Twitter instead of booze, and living their
emotional life online. I suppose this all comes under the rubric
of The Way We Live Now. But why does it all seem so arid, so less
than enticing?

The Internet, in its ability to punish through so-called social
media, is of course a great aid to political correctness, and political correctness is another enemy of the novel. The ethnic and
gender strait-jacketing of political correctness is by its very nature
opposed to the premise that the great novelist or story writer can

imagine the lives of all people at any time. And so once they could. For the novelist, freedom of speech extended to freedom of imagination. Now, under political correctness, both imagination and expression have been severely curtailed. Nowadays a white novelist who writes a book about a black man or woman, or even with significant black or women characters in it, is headed for trouble, as William Styron discovered as long ago as 1967 when he published *The Confessions of Nat Turner*, his novel about the slave revolt of 1831 in Virginia. Today, as a white southerner, Styron, were he alive, would likely not have had the temerity to take on the subject. Today, owing to political correctness, any novelist would be in instant trouble if he or she were even to impute bad motives to any of his characters who were members of minority groups. In the current day, is it even possible to have a male novelist write favorably about a female heroine, a white about a black, a heterosexual about a homosexual? The Nobel Prize–winning novelist Kazuo Ishiguro has spoken to the "climate of fear" among writers that political correctness has wrought, leaving writers worried that "an anonymous lynch mob will turn up online and make their lives a misery." Ishiguro told an interviewer that "I very much fear for the younger generation of writers" and that "I think this is a dangerous state of affairs."

Apparently the scourge of political correctness has now seeped down to young adult fiction. So strong are the precepts of political correctness enforced in the realm of young adult fiction that not even J. K. Rowling, she of the *Harry Potter* novels, is invulnerable to them. Ms. Rowling was strongly criticized for a 2020 essay in which she argued that the rights of transgender people be balanced with the rights of women. For this she was condemned as a "TERF" (a trans-exclusionary radical feminist), someone who doesn't consider transgender women as real women, and hence politically incorrect. At the firm that publishes Rowling's *Harry Potter* books, a number of PC employees refused to work on *The*

Ickabog, her most recent book. So severe are these strictures, these attacks on free expression, that many authors of young adult fiction are said to have abandoned the field entirely.

Political correctness, if its rampages on the culture are allowed to continue to go unchecked, also figures to destroy the criticism of novels, and, for that matter, much else in the cultural and educational realms. How can a man possibly criticize the novel of a woman, a white criticize that of a black, a straight that of a gay writer? The larger point is that political correctness makes large segments of the culture no longer open to honest discussion. The politically correct consensus has it, as the biracial English novelist Zadie Smith wrote, "that we can and should write only about people who are fundamentally like us: racially, sexually, genetically, politically, personally. That only an intimate authorial autobiographical connection with a character can be the rightful basis of a fiction." As a true writer, Zadie Smith finds this catastrophic.

As we have seen, the best novelists have always taken the whole world and all its denizens for their domain. Often they have been, in their literary scope, impressively androgynous. The narrator of Willa Cather's *My Ántonia* is a young man. In *Death Comes for the Archbishop*, Cather chose to write not about two nuns but about two priests. If you were to read either of these novels absent dust-jackets or title pages, you could not tell whether it was written by a man or woman. Henry James did men and women with equal aplomb, and so often did Edith Wharton. Two of the greatest female characters in literature, Anna Karenina and Natasha Rostova, were created by Leo Tolstoy. In *Daniel Deronda*, George Eliot, a gentile, wrote one of the first novels with a Zionist theme, with Jewish characters who are utterly convincing, and Eliot was able to create both men and women characters with equal artistic aplomb. Sad to think all these writers might be hesitant to attempt their dazzling characters in our day.

Under the reign of political correctness, "appropriation" is the name given to writing about things outside one's own gender or ethnicity or even milieu. A writer is no longer permitted to "appropriate" the material of those to whom presumably by rights it belongs, leaving only what is legitimately available to the writer his or her own exclusive experience and no one else's. The novelist Lionel Shriver—a female Lionel, in the event you do not know of her—caused a stir when she rightly complained that the ideologies behind "appropriation" would put an end to all fiction. "The ultimate endpoint of keeping our mitts off experience that *doesn't belong to us*," Shriver writes, "is that there is no fiction.... All that's left is memoir." Like the man said, just the facts—leave imagination at the door.

Perhaps not all that surprisingly, novels are now being published whose outlook is dominated by this same political correctness. In the journal *Liberties* Becca Rothfeld calls them "Sanctimony Literature," in an essay by the same name. These novels are notable for their clear but also crude morality; they are peopled by good guys and bad, the difference between them easily established by their political views. The heroes and heroines in these novels have all the right opinions, and detest those who do not share them. They are ardent about climate change, more than O.K. with transgenderism, and propelled by a loathing for capitalism. Becca Rothfeld writes: "Sanctimony literature errs, then, not because it ventures into moral territory, but because it displays no genuine curiosity about what it really means to be good, and is blind to the distinction between morality and moralism, and exhibits no doubt about its own probity."

After examining three of these sanctimony novels in her essay, Rothfeld writes: "The heroes and heroines of sanctimony literature are so steeped in self-satisfaction that they provide an inadvertent moral lesson. It turns out that someone can have all the *de rigueur* political opinions without thereby achieving any measure of meaningful ethical success. A novel's goodness *is* bound up with its beauty, but there is more to goodness than boilerplate leftist fervor... The sanctimonists maintain a tidily bifurcated interest in good people and bad people, when in fact what they should be studying is the good and the bad in all people—the full murk of human motivation, the tangle of tensions and contradictions, of desires and principles, that is the permanent condition of human choice." That condition has also been the domain of the best literary artists, and goes back as far as antiquity when Euripides, in his *Aeolus*, wrote:

> Virtue and vice ne'er separately exist,
> But in the same acts with each other twist.

The critic Lionel Trilling long ago made the crucial distinction between moral realism and moral righteousness. Moral realism attempts to establish morality in what is often its daunting complexity, while moral righteousness is content to reside in its own sense of self-superiority. As a character in the Bernard Malamud story "A Choice of Profession" says, "It's not easy being moral." Being moralistic, on the other hand, is no problem whatsoever; it entails no more than assuming your own virtue and the foolishness of anyone who disagrees with you.

On the matter of moral action in fiction, one of the chief dramas played out in serious novels is that of the struggle not only to establish what is good, but to be good. Rothfeld mentions in this connection the character Viktor Struhm in Vasily Grossman's powerful novel *Life and Fate*, who struggles to live honorably under the pressure of Soviet totalitarianism, as well as Jane Austen's Elizabeth Bennett's ardor for correct judgment in *Pride and Prejudice*, which is of course really a novel about the difficulty of rising above both pride and prejudice. One could name several other novels whose theme is the complexity of morality and whose characters fight to attain the moral life in balanced measure. An argument could be made—I have tried from time to time here to make it—that this is what the novel at its best does.

Of the sanctimony novels Rothfeld examines, two are set in universities, and one in a high school. Doubtless they are the work of writers who themselves have been trained in one of what is said to be more 350 extant university "creative writing" programs, at the end of which one receives an MFA, and, if one is lucky, gets a job teaching other aspiring novelists and poets, who if they themselves are lucky will land similar jobs. (And so the beat, as the old disc jockeys had it, goes on.) In the courses in these programs one writes stories and poems that are "workshopped," which is to say intricately discussed by one's instructors and fellow students. ("If there's one word that sums up everything that's gone wrong since the war," remarked Kingsley Amis, "it's Workshop. After Youth, that is.") The results of all this "workshopping" in producing important writers has been less than impressive. In the current day, given the heavy atmosphere of political correctness in universities, the result may well be even less impressive than formerly in the years ahead.

Academic life, which often turns out to be the subject of so much fiction turned out by men and women who have MFA degrees, has not been fertile ground for the novel. A small number of good novels with an academic background have been pro- duced—Amis's *Lucky Jim*, David Lodge's *Changing Places*, John Williams's *Stoner*, C. P. Snow's *The Masters*—most of these satiriz- ing the academic life, its petty concerns, its disappointed deni- zens, its dreary love affairs. But perhaps the chief criticism to be made about academically trained novelists is that their time in the university—either as students or (as many go on to be) teachers— takes them out of the world, the larger world where the great sub- jects for the novel are to be found. All that the academic novelist is left to write about is the high intensity of academic disputes (so high is it, as Henry Kissinger is famously said to have remarked, "because the stakes are so low,") and the dullish love affairs with students that some years ago seem to have been among the perks of the professoriate.

Here, from a review in the *Nation*, is a summary of two recent academic novels: Christine Smallwood's debut novel, *The Life of the Mind*, and Lynn Steger Strong's second novel, *Want*:

> In *The Life of the Mind*, we meet Dorothy, a PhD living in "adjunct hell." She teaches "two or three or sometimes four" English courses at the same New York City university where she earned her doctorate. In between classes, she tries to "write the sample chapter that would get her the [book] contract that would get her the job that didn't exist." In *Want*, we meet another struggling adjunct, who has a lighter teaching load—only one course a week—but, in typical adjunct fashion, also has a second job, as a teacher at a charter high school. Only part of the book explores her work as an adjunct, but this is entirely appropriate: She's a part-time academic, earning a fraction of a full-time professor's pay. When she's introduced to the wealthy couples who have hired her husband, a carpenter, to build closets or cabinets in their Long Island homes, she struggles to explain her career to them: She's a professor, "except no health insurance." She calls herself a "professor of failing to find a way to make a living wage."

If this doesn't dampen your appetite, here is a further paragraph from the same review:

> *The Life of the Mind* begins with an ending—specifically, with an ending that just won't end. It's the final week of March, and Dorothy is shitting and bleeding in a university bathroom stall. She's having a miscarriage and has been hemorrhaging for six

days straight. She hadn't chosen to end the pregnancy, nor had she made the conscious decision to keep it. She had learned the fetus was no longer viable and jump-started its expulsion by administering misoprostol. Observing her blood—"thick, curdled knots of string, gelatinous in substance"—and avoiding calls from one of her two therapists, Dorothy wonders when the miscarriage truly began. "She would never know when it exactly had happened—when it had stopped happening—only that she had persisted for some time idly believing that she was persisting, her body busy fulfilling its potential like some warehouse or shipping center. How typical of her not to know something was over when it was over," Smallwood writes in the close third person, with occasional forays into free indirect style. It's hard to say what "it" even is: "When she self-administered the uterine evacuation, terminating a—what was it, exactly? What did you call it when a life stopped developing, but didn't end?"

To parody an early rock 'n' roll song, roll over, Tolstoy, and tell Dostoyevsky the news: the academic novel, pray God, is not here to stay, though I fear it is.

What novels are "here to stay" becomes a more and more complex question as contemporary publishing itself becomes more complex. Publishing, once thought an arm of literature, has in recent years began to resemble a rejecting finger. Publishers in the past have made famous mistakes in turning down great books. André Gide, then at *Nouvelle Revue Française* in Paris, turned down Marcel Proust's *Swann's Way*, and an editor at another French firm in his rejection letter wrote to Proust: "My dear friend, perhaps I am dense, but I just don't understand why a man should take thirty pages to describe how he turns over in bed before he goes to sleep. It made my head swim." In England, T. S. Eliot, then working at the firm of Faber & Faber, turned down *Animal Farm*, which over the years cost Faber & Faber millions of lost dollars. *A Confederacy of Dunces*, a novel by John Kennedy Toole that in 1981 won the Pulitzer Prize, is said to have been rejected by fourteen publishers. One could write an interesting essay on famous publishers' rejections, and an accompanying one on the vast publishers' advances paid to authors of books that, deservedly, found few readers.

In an earlier day, though, publishers did not so insistently ask, as they now seem regularly to do, if a book will show a profit. Rupert Hart-Davis, the English editor, though happy enough to show a profit on any book he published, wrote to his former teacher and friend George Lyttelton: "It's usually impossible to forecast what books are going to sell, unless the author already has a steady public. I always assume that anything I particularly like will not sell at all, but publish it nevertheless. If one abandons one's own opinion in the attempt to gauge the market, one is lost indeed."

Hart-Davis ran his own publishing firm and so had the freedom to publish based on his preferences, not on his commercial instincts. Fewer and fewer contemporary editors are in the same position. Studies appear from time to time that reveal roughly the same number of books get published and then sold (which assumes they are read). A few novelists whose first two or three books fail to sell in decent numbers find it impossible to find publishers at all. The critic Joseph Bottum, in his *Decline of the Novel*, wrote about the "Cocktail Party Test" for fiction, which asked whether or not it was necessary to have read a current novel to pass for being oneself *au courant*. The last such novel, Bottum maintains, was Tom Wolfe's *Bonfire of the Vanities*, published in 1987. Publishers continue to publish fiction, but, apart from publishing the few living novelist who retain a reputation, one sometimes wonders why. I myself read fewer and fewer contemporary novels, though I do check the publication of new novels in the weekly fiction section of the London *Times Literary Supplement*, and not many of the novels reviewed there seem, to me at least,

promising. Here, to cite a single egregious example, is the opening
of an August 17, 2018, review of a novel with the title *Come Join Our
Disease* by Sam Byers:

> In Ottessa Moshfegh's novel *My Year of Rest and Relaxation*, the
> narrator defecates on the floor of the gallery where she works: it
> is a farewell "fuck you" to employment and civil society as much
> as it is a comment on contemporary art. This dirty protest is
> positively quaint, however, in comparison with the scatological
> activism of Byers' third novel (brace yourself):
>> I brought the wadded chuck of bread round to my backside,
>> pressed it into the cleft of my buttocks, and drew it as firmly
>> as I could across my anus to wipe myself... And then, as a
>> gesture, a statement, I bit into the shit-smeared bread and
>> swallowed it down.

Pause here to block this out of one's mind, hopefully forever.

More and more aspiring novelists and short-story writers,
unwanted at once-thought-to-be-literary publishing houses, are
self-publishing. Self-publishing means these writers count on the
Internet for word of their work to get around. One cannot but
wish them well, hoping that some few among them have written
novels that will enrich the lives of those who read them. But the
old excitement of the novel—its publication date, reviews of it in
important periodicals, critical discussion of it, yes, even its standing in the Cocktail Party Test—appears to be leaching away.

Then there is the phenomenon known as "graphic novels." I
put quotation marks around the term because many of those who
produce them are quite content with their work being called what
they believe it is: comic books. The critic Daniel Raeburn writes: "I
snicker at the neologism first for its insecure pretension—the literary equivalent of calling a garbage man a 'sanitation engineer'—
and second because a 'graphic novel' is in fact the very thing it is

ashamed to admit: a comic book, rather than a comic pamphlet or comic magazine." The chief difference between a graphic novel and a comic book, it has been said, is the binding. Neil Gaiman, who has also written for the movies and television and thinks of himself as writing comic books and not graphic novels, upon hearing the term graphic novel remarked, "I felt like someone who'd been informed that she wasn't actually a hooker; that in fact she was a lady of the evening."

Like so many kids of my generation, I grew up on comic books—on *Superman, Batman, Captain Marvel, Wonder Woman, Archie,* and others—which comprised my first enthusiastic reading. A bit later, in the final years of grade school and then in the early years of high school I read a fair amount of what were then known as Classic Comics, or comic books drawn from nineteenth-century novels that had adventurous turns and twists—those by Dickens, Dumas, James Fenimore Cooper, etc. These were also useful for faking that regular dreary school exercise of the day known as the book report. Instead of reading a lengthy novel, I read a Classic Comic version of the novel, and reported on it as if I had read the four- or five-hundred-page version of the actual novel. I was never caught out on the deception.

The first I had heard of graphic novels was sometime in the 1980s, when Art Spiegelman published *Maus,* a work about his father's experience in the Holocaust and his own life as the son of a Holocaust survivor, which originally appeared in an avant-garde comic and graphics magazine called *Raw,* published by Spiegelman and his wife. I knew that graphic novels had become more popular over the years, but I hadn't realized the growth in their pretension until I recently noted a full section in my local library devoted to them. And then not long ago two thick graphic novel volumes showed up in my mail purporting to be the first two volumes of Marcel Proust's *In Search of Lost Time*: *Swann's Way* and *In the Shadow of Young Girls in Flower.* A comic-book version of

Proust—who would have thought it? Not even the nervy kid that I was at fourteen would have attempted to pan that off in one of my phony book reports.

A less likely candidate for cartooning than Proust's complex novel is not easily imagined. No comic-book balloon could be large enough to accommodate 99 percent of Proust's sinuous, one is almost inclined to say *zaftig*, sentences. This greatest of all novelists of the interior life is not about to be captured by cartoon characters modeled on the carefully drawn literary portraiture, above all on the self-portraiture, that is at the heart of *In Search of Lost Time*. While it is faintly amusing to have cartoon faces of the Baron de Charlus and the Duchesse de Guermantes drawn by the artist Stéphane Heuet, no draughtsman could hope to capture the subtlety of the character of the Baron or of the Duchesse. Besides, their faces are better left to the imagination of the true novel's readers. Jane Austen never describes Elizabeth Bennett, the heroine of *Pride and Prejudice*, thus allowing every young woman reading the novel to think Miss Bennett looks like her and thereby increasing the element of identification.

Eager to find the justification for a graphic novel version of Proust's great novel, I read its translator Arthur Goldhammer's introduction with equal measures of interest and skepticism. Professor Goldhammer, whose translations from the French have won prizes both in France and in the United States, argues that the graphic novel version of *In Search of Lost Time* might form "a gentle introduction" to the formidable—and for many the forbidding—work that is Proust's novel. In other words, more than three-hundred pages of comic book (roughly the length of Proust's first volumes in their graphic novel version) might ease the way into reading the work as Proust wrote it. Goldhammer also claims that "the ruthless compression required to squeeze Proust's expansive sentences into "confining frames" yields the benefit of shedding "a revealing light on the armature, on the columns, pillars, and arches

that support the narrator's resurrected memories as the columns
of the church in Combray support the stained glass and tapes-
tries that transport visitors into the past they represent." Professor
Goldhammer goes on to argue that even those who have read the
novel "may make new discoveries thanks to the clarity of what
might be likened to a piano reduction to an orchestral score." He
adds that what is really being offered here is "*un menu degustation*,
or tasting menu, [that] tries to give a full sampling of the dishes in
the repertoire of a great chef."

Ingenious, really, this explanation, and so much more elaborate than my own coarse speculation about why a serious translator would take on such a hopeless project as a comic book Proust.
Reading Professor Goldhammer's introduction, I recall many
years ago attending a lecture by Stephen Potter, the English paro-
dist of self-help books, who, at the lecture's end, was asked by an
earnest graduate student why he, Potter, an acknowledged scholar
of Samuel Taylor Coleridge, would bother to write such works as
Gamesmanship, *Lifemanship*, and *Supermanship*. Potter hesitated,
emphatically cleared his throat, and in a distinctly U English
accent, announced, "Out of work, you know."

Doubtless there are people who have good, even significant
stories to tell and who are better able to tell them through pic-
tures than through words. Art Spiegelman may be such a person.
Doubtless, too, many people do not have the *sitzfleisch*, or bottom
patience, to work their way through lengthy novels of great psychological penetration such as Marcel Proust offers. Graphic novels, a case could be made, are for them better than no novels at all.
But what also cannot be doubted is that graphic novels, however
artfully done, cannot replace, because they cannot perform at the
same level of complexity, what I have been calling serious novels,
and so they represent a radical dumbing down and as such join the
list of enemies of the novel.

The Internet and digital culture, political correctness, creative

writing programs, the state of contemporary publishing, and
graphic novels have put the fate of the novel in peril, but perhaps the most subtly pernicious enemy of the novel may be what
Philip Rieff, in an important 1966 book, called *The Triumph of the
Therapeutic*. This triumph, Rieff argued, marked a significant shift
in our culture. In his book Rieff contended that we are no longer
living in a culture where honor and dignity, courage and kindness,
are primary, but instead in one in which self-esteem and self-grat-
ification are the chief goals. The enemy in the new therapeutic culture is repression, and its main means of expression is confession.

One sees evidence of the triumph of the therapeutic everywhere in current-day life. In the raising of children, it now reigns
supreme, with every child thought to be a fragile being, whose
mental balance must be protected in every possible way. In education, the classroom, from kindergarten through university, has
begun more and more to resemble the therapy session. College
students openly declare themselves feeling unsafe in the pres-
ence of ideas with which they do not agree, and professors accede
to their fears by providing trigger-warnings or simply agreeing
not to touch on subjects that might upset them. Even in sports,
coaches talk about players bonding, about losses being learning
experiences, about teams "growing"; more and more, psychobab-
ble is the order of the day. Athletes themselves, men above six-
foot seven and weighing more than three hundred pounds, openly
weep on television after losing, or for that matter after winning,
a game. Why hold back one's fears, tears, insecurities? Under the
reign of the therapeutic culture, there is no longer any need to do
so; in fact, to do so is felt to be wrong. It's O.K. Don't hold back.
Let it all out.

To be sure, vast is the pain that psychotherapy, greatly aided in
recent decades by pharmacology, has relieved, making life livable
for those suffering schizophrenia and bipolar disease, and others born with genetic mis-wirings. Intelligent psychotherapy has

also been useful in propping up those depressed and otherwise defeated by the misfortunes life has visited upon them. Much can be said about the value of psychotherapy generally, but its toll on literature, and especially on the novel, has been heavy.

Great literature is about the role of destiny and moral conflict. The therapeutic culture is about individual happiness. Some novelists have been deeply affected—others would say "infected"—by Freud, Jung, and other sires of the therapeutic culture. One thinks here of Henry Roth, whose novel *Call It Sleep*, published as long ago as 1934, would appear to have been written according to a Freudian program. Other novelists have been highly suspicious of the therapeutic culture generally and Freudian psychology in particular. Vladimir Nabokov rarely passed up a chance to refer to Sigmund Freud as "the Viennese quack." The argument against Freudian psychology for the novelist is against its narrowing and predeterminate explanations of human behavior. For many therapeutic thinkers—for Freud, Karen Horney, and others—all the important cards are dealt early in life, in our infancy, our fate determined by the nature of our breast-feeding or maternal intimacy. For Freud, who claimed to have taken his insights from the poets, the Oedipus Complex must be resolved—too bad that, in his literary reading, the old boy didn't take a pass on Sophocles—and sex was the central fact of the human condition.

Under the reign of therapy triumphant, the goal of self-esteem has replaced the longing for strong character. The essayist Anthony Daniels, who is also a psychiatrist, has written, apropos of the new dominance of therapeutic culture, that "every bad decision that people made was attributed to lack of self-esteem, rather than to such human phenomena as, say, weakness, folly, cowardice, laziness, or even fear or duress, the first four of which were dismissed as being incurably *judgmental* and therefore useless as scientific explanation." The problem with self-esteem, Daniels goes on to explain, is that "it is entirely egotistical and self-regarding, unlike self-respect, which is a social virtue and imposes discipline and obligations upon the person who has, or wishes to have, it. By contrast, self-esteem is like a medal that one pins to one's own chest merely by virtue of existing. I am, therefore I esteem myself, and I demand that you esteem me too."

For the true novelist, self-esteem and so much else in the therapeutic realm is tosh. Life is more complex than the analyses and panaceas of the therapist or the dreams of future happiness of his patients. Fate, that great trickster, offers no couch for the resolution of life's problems. Morality is richer than any fifty-minute session, even twelve years of such sessions, can hope to comprehend. Surely Proust, in this single sentence, came closer to the truth of human existence than all of therapeutic culture: "We do not receive wisdom, we must discover it for ourselves, after a journey which no one else can make for us, and no one can spare us."¶

XIV.

WHAT WE HOPE FROM A NOVEL is that, somehow, reading it will broaden our experience, sharpen our perceptions, make us a bit wiser about the world. As David Cecil has it, "No one person can ever know in practice what it is to be both a man and woman, a mystic and a materialist, a criminal and a pillar of society, an ancient Roman and a modern Russian." No one person, I would only add, but perhaps Leo Tolstoy, who never did a Roman character, perhaps because Shakespeare, the praise of whom he, Tolstoy, never understood, did so many.

My current reading happens to be a nearly seven-hundred-page book titled *Great Short Works of Leo Tolstoy*. The book includes nine stories, a few of them—"The Cossacks," "The Kreutzer Sonata," "Hadji Murad"—long enough to be considered novellas. Tolstoy was, in my view, the greatest of novelists, perhaps the greatest writer of all time and among all genres. Every character he created comes alive, every novel and story he wrote stirs one's imagination, making one want to read on to learn how things will come out for the people he has created. His beginnings hook one, his endings do not disappoint, and everything between these beginnings and endings, every detail, holds one's attention. Even his *longueurs*—as many consider the segments on history in *War and Peace*—are of interest. While reading him one cannot imagine why one would ever wish to read anyone else.

Consider "The Kreutzer Sonata," a story of obsession, of love gone sour, of jealousy leading to murder. The story is told to a narrator who is on a lengthy train journey by the man seated next to him who underwent the loss of marital love and ended by murdering his wife out of jealousy. Tolstoy being Tolstoy, the story, as I have just blatantly laid it out, is about much more than the tale of a fiercely jealous and disappointed husband. Encountered along the way are endless observations and aphorisms, *aperçus* and insights, considerations of the place of women as the object of male lust, of the reliance upon and false authority of medicine, the hopelessness of modern psychology, the effects of music on the psyche, the "mad beast of jealousy," and much more.

"The Kreutzer Sonata" is not among the greatest of Tolstoy's stories, but reading it is the intellectual equivalent of a splendid workout at the gym—one feels better for having undergone it. Tolstoy, who had strong views and in his later works was given to preaching, nevertheless forces one to consider one's own views on the most basic of subjects: the arrangements of marriage, the place of women, the nature of love, and many others. Reading his "Kreutzer Sonata," one never feels less than imaginatively, intellectually, spiritually engaged.

The protagonist of "The Kreutzer Sonata," Pozdnyshev, the man who on a train trip recounts his love for and eventual murder of his wife, remarks of music:

"They say that music exalts the soul. Nonsense, it is not true!
It has an effect, an awful effect—I am speaking of myself—but
not of an exalting kind. It has neither an exalting nor a debasing
effect but it produces agitation. How can I put it? Music makes
me forget myself, my real position; it transports me to some
other position not my own. Under the influence of music it
seems to me that I feel what I do not really feel, understand what
I do not understand, that I can do what I cannot do."

The background to these remarks is that Pozdnyshev's wife has taken for a lover a violinist with whom she plays Beethoven's Violin Sonata No. 9, for piano and violin, "the Kreutzer," and it is this music that stirs the intimacy between them, and gets her betrayal of Pozdnyshev underway.

Does this situation, Pozdnyshev's wife's beginning an affair with the violinist, detract from, or even lessen, the cogency of his account of the ultimately deranging effects of music? How high is the truth quotient of that account? Is it merely a thought Tolstoy put into the head of his character, or did he himself believe it? Tolstoy published the story in 1890, rather late in his literary career, when in many ways he had turned puritanical in his thinking. (For Tolstoy at his most stringently puritanical, see his "Why Do Men Stupefy Themselves?," where he comes out against alcohol, tobacco, most arrangements of society, and much else.) And why should it matter if Tolstoy believed these severe strictures about music? Yet, somehow, it does matter—because he is Tolstoy and not subject to trivial thoughts.

One of the effects of reading Pozdnyshev (or is it Tolstoy?) on music is to cause the reader—as it certainly caused this reader—to argue with it. Beethoven, Tolstoy has Pozdnyshev say, wrote the Kreutzer because he was in a "condition" that "caused him to do certain actions and therefore that condition had a meaning for him, but for me—none at all. That is why music only agitates and doesn't lead to a conclusion." That music doesn't lead to a conclusion is true enough, but that it only agitates isn't true, either, though it might be true of some of Beethoven's stormier music. The cantatas of Bach, the flute and the piano quartets and concertos of Mozart, the quintets and songs of Schubert, and so much more from the vast treasure house of music, far from always agitating, more often becalms, reminding one of the elevated states possible to humankind. Well, one could go on arguing with Pozdnyshev-Tolstoy, as I did in my mind off and on for a day or so after reading

"The Kreutzer Sonata," but, then, this is what great fiction does: it turns facts into ideas, where they, the ideas, seem so much more vivid than when standing alone.

For a stellar case of knowing where a novelist stands, one perhaps cannot come up with a stronger and yet more ambiguous example than Ivan Turgenev's *Fathers and Sons* (1862). This is a novel about the irremediable conflict between strong political views: between traditional views of nineteenth-century Russian liberalism and the views of a radical younger generation. As Isaiah Berlin wrote in his introduction to a twentieth-century edition of the novel: "The central topic of the novel is the confrontation of the old and the young, of liberals and radicals, traditional civilization and the new, harsh positivism which has no use for anything except what is needed by a rational man."

This conflict is set out in Turgenev's creation of the gentry Kirsanov family and the young physician Yvegeny Bazarov, whose impatience with existing social arrangements and intolerance of all efforts at ameliorating them is at the center of his being, a figure who has been described as an adumbration of the Bolsheviks well before they uprooted Russian life. Clear though the delineation of both sides in *Fathers and Sons* is, you cannot read the novel without wondering which side the novel's author was on—and, if you aren't already entirely committed in your politics, which side you yourself are on.

At its publication, *Fathers and Sons* was attacked from both sides. In its day the novel divided rooms, readers loving or hating it according to their own political views. Many viewed Turgenev's portrayal of his character Bazarov as an attack on the younger generation in Russia; others viewed it as an attack on the Russian nobility. Dostoyevsky had no difficulty in locating Turgenev's true sentiments. In his novel *The Possessed*, he has a character named Semyon Yegorovich Karmazinov, a pathetically vain literary man clearly modeled on Turgenev who is portrayed as shamelessly

sucking up to the youthful nihilists of the day—Turgenev coined
the term nihilist—who are the main characters in the novel.
Turgenev would later write that "with the exception of his
views on art, I share almost all of Bazarov's other convictions." But
in the composition of his novel, Turgenev, as his biographer Henri
Troyat writes, "had tried to be impartial," adding: "His main idea
was that an artist should not set out to prove anything—he could
show, suggest, light the way, but not pass judgments upon his characters' personality or acts." But even this view, that of impartiality,
is often thought unsuitable among the politically committed. "All
his life," Isaiah Berlin writes of Turgenev, "he wished to march with
the progressives, with the party of liberty and protest. But, in the
end, he could not bring himself to accept their brutal contempt
for art, civilized behavior, for everything he held dear in European
culture." To this day the debate among readers of *Fathers and Sons*
continues: Is Bazarov a character we should condemn, a precur-
sor of the brutes who, under the banner of Communism, loosed
utter mayhem and committed major massacres, or ought his cool
scientific outlook and idealism to be admired, himself viewed as a
beacon of enlightened values?

Fathers and Sons, and other political novels written long
after it, ask if we, as readers, can surmount our own politics in
the name of a more complex, a higher truth than politics itself
permits. Sometimes these politics are deliberate, as in the cases of
such more recent novelists as Nelson Algren and E. L. Doctorow,
who wrote unequivocally as men of the Left, wishing to make
political arguments through their novels. Ayn Rand, from the
Right, did much the same, though, given the extraordinary
commercial success of *Atlas Shrugged* and *The Fountainhead*,
doubtless to better effect. In *The Possessed*, Dostoyevsky wrote to
satirize the pretensions of leftist dreams of an earthly utopia, and
in doing so brilliantly foretold the coming of totalitarianism in
the twentieth century.

Stendhal famously remarked that "politics in a work of literature is like a pistol-shot in the middle of a concert, something loud
and vulgar, and yet a thing to which it is not possible to ignore." In
fiction politics can of course be immensely seductive. Not above
such seduction myself, I have long thought Saul Bellow's best
novel *Mr. Sammler's Planet* (1970), while wondering how much
this is owing to my sharing the book's protagonist's (and, I believe,
Bellow's own) cultural politics, which entail an antipathy to the
student protest movement of the 1960s, a belief in the fragility of
civilization, a suspicion of the sort of idealism that comes at no
expense to those who claim it, and a reverence for the great writers
of the past, however dead, white, or European they may be.

Perhaps the most astute political novel of all comes from
that most apolitical of writers, Henry James. In *The Princess
Casamassima* (1885–86), James creates characters of various
political perspectives and persuasions—from activist radicals to
radical chic aristocrats to true victims of social oppression. But
it is a secondary character in the novel, Madame Grandoni, who
speaks for James when she announces: "An honorable nature, of
any class, I always respect; but I won't pretend to a passion for
the ignorant masses, for I have it not." As the novel proceeds,
Hyacinth Robinson, the poor orphan who is at the center of the
book, discovers that there are values higher than social equality;
he develops an aesthetic sense and comes to realize that it would
make no sense to divide up the magnificent St. Mark's cathedral in
Venice among the people. Hyacinth Robinson will eventually take
his own life, but before doing so he will also recognize that politics isn't what life is truly about. As another character in the novel
remarks: "The figures on the chessboard were still the passions
and jealousies and superstitions and stupidities of man, and thus
positioned with regard to each other at any given moment could
be of interest only to the grim fates who played the game—who
sat, through the ages, bow-backed over the table." In other words,

for Henry James, and for the novel at its best generally, politics isn't where the action truly is.

The case against tendentiousness in the novel is nicely stated by the novelist and critic Cynthia Ozick: "When a thesis or a framework—any kind of prescriptiveness or tendentiousness—is imposed on the writing of fiction, imagination flies out the door, and with it the freedom and volatility and irresponsibility that imagination both confers and commands." Lionel Shriver, who writes journalism as well as fiction, has noted that "fiction is much more subtle. It's more evasive, it's more circuitous, it should be a little harder to discern what the message is—not that it shouldn't have a message, but that message is usually complex and sometimes contradictory." Esau sold his birthright, it will be recalled, for a mess of pottage, but the politically tendentious novelist is willing to sell his or hers for a pot of message.

So widely do even great novels range in their differences that in considering them one finds only exceptions that prove no rules. I think here of Joseph Conrad, a novelist long firmly residing in my own personal pantheon of great writers. Some of Conrad's most powerful novels—*The Secret Agent*, *Under Western Eyes*, and *Nostromo*—along with his perhaps most famous because most taught work—his novella *Heart of Darkness*—are political and, it could be argued, tendentious into the bargain. Yet Joseph Conrad somehow rises above even his own strong politics to create works of enduring art.

But, then, nearly everything about Joseph Conrad was exceptional. He wrote, at great pain, in English, his third language. He began writing in earnest in his thirties, and did not publish his first novel, *Alymayer's Folly*, until he was thirty-eight. He revered Henry James and loathed Dostoyevsky for what he took to be his savage Russianness. Conrad was, in effect, orphaned by Russia. His father, Apollo Korzeniowski, was a Polish nationalist and hence a revolutionist attempting to free his country from Tsarist control.

He was captured and along with his wife and their five-year-old
son was sent into exile in a province north of Moscow, where
his mother died of tuberculosis; his father would later also die of
tuberculosis, when Conrad was eleven. He never lost his hatred of
Russia and things Russian; the hatred is on display in his novels
The Secret Agent and *Under Western Eyes.*

In his fiction Joseph Conrad managed to rise above his personal views in his search for universal truths, knowing that they
could only be found through careful investigation of the particular.
Perhaps for this reason Conrad refused to read Freud, remarking
that "I do not want to reach the *depths.* I want to treat reality like
a raw and rough object which I touch with my fingers." One won't
find anything resembling traditional love stories in Joseph Conrad.
Zdzisław Najder, his best biographer, writes: "I believe that Conrad
opposed the emphasis on erotic themes in literature because he
was convinced that it would overshadow more vital and serious
problems. Among the subjects that concerned him most—responsibility, the sense of duty, guilt, justice, freedom, honor, solidar-
ity, anarchy, order—masculine-feminine affairs were not in the
forefront." Love of life itself was one of his themes. As Axel Heyst,
the lonely protagonist of Conrad's novel *Victory,* after fighting off
the philosophical nihilism taught him by his father, puts it: "Ah,
Davidson, woe to the man whose heart has not learned when
young to hope, to love—and to put its trust in life."

If Joseph Conrad may be said to have had a politics, they were
a conservative love of tradition and order combined with a hatred
of injustice. In later years he would be mistakenly taken for a racist
and a right-wing reactionary, when in fact he was anti-imperialist
and a critic of empty white supremacy (see *Heart of Darkness* and
Nostromo passim). He was a writer who sensed perhaps more than
anyone of his time the fragility of civilization, and through his fiction he exposed the many ways it could be betrayed. His were the
politics of the true novelist, which is to say, the politics above all

politics, dedicated instead to the complex truth of life itself. In his fiction Conrad explored the most serious questions: Why do the wicked often flourish? Why is justice delayed and sometimes never dispensed at all? Why do many of the innocent suffer? And he explored them in ways both complex and compelling.

The best novels are not, should not be, tendentious, expressing or promoting a special cause or program, no matter how worthy that cause or program. This includes the politically, the theologically, even the racially tendentious. Beyond doubt the most important novel published in the United States—important in its effect—has been Harriet Beecher Stowe's *Uncle Tom's Cabin*. "So you are the little woman who started this great war," Abraham Lincoln is alleged—apparently falsely—to have said to Mrs. Stowe upon meeting her. Important though *Uncle Tom's Cabin* was, its importance remains historical only. To be sure, touches of tendentiousness show up in Dickens, in Tolstoy, in George Eliot, and in other great novelists, but the capaciousness of their novels does not permit the tendentious bits, the message portions, to spoil them. "You want messages," Samuel Goldwyn is supposed to have said, "go to Western Union." That, for the novelist, is probably still good advice.

Not that novelists need shy away from ideas. But, to cite Desmond MacCarthy again, the novelist's job is not to begin with ideas but to "turn facts into ideas." Willa Cather was splendid at doing precisely this. As an example, in her novel *The Professor's House* we in effect overhear the eponymous professor, Godfrey St. Peter, in his classroom, tell a student

"No, Miller, I don't myself think much of science as a phase of human development. It has given us a lot of ingenious toys; they take our attention away from the real problems, of course, and since the problems are insoluble, I suppose we ought to be grateful for distraction. But the fact is, the human mind,

the individual mind, has always been made more interesting
by dwelling on the old riddles, even if makes nothing of them.
Science hasn't given us any new amazement, except of the super-
ficial kind we get from witnessing dexterity and slight-of-hand.
It hasn't given us any richer pleasures, as the Renaissance did,
nor any new sins—not one! . . . It is the laboratory, not the Lamb
of God, that taketh away the sins of the world. . . . I don't think
you help people by making their conduct of no importance—
you impoverish them. As long as every man and woman who
crowded into the cathedrals on Easter Sunday was a principal
in a gorgeous drama with God, glittering angels on one side
and the shadows of evil coming and going on the other, life was
a rich thing. The king and the beggar had the same chance at
miracles and great temptations and revelations. And that's what
makes men happy, believing in the mystery and importance of
their own individual lives. It makes us happy to surround our
creature needs and bodily instincts with as much pomp and
circumstance as possible. Art and religion (they are the same
thing in the end, of course) have given man the only happiness
he has ever had."

Consider only the final sentence of that brilliant passage. How it
coaxes us to delve further into its meaning. Are art and religion
really the same thing? Have they alone brought men and women
their only happiness? If so, how so? And has there ever been a
human drama to compete with that of salvation in an afterlife?
Cather's novels have many such fetching observations, all put in
the mouths or minds of complex and utterly believable characters.
"Desire is creation," thinks Professor St. Peter, "is the magic element in that process." Elsewhere he notes his fight at his own university against those forces whose aim in education was to "show
results," an aim "that was undermining and vulgarizing education."
What, precisely, is wrong with showing results in education? One

has to ponder the matter. Tom Outland, the other chief figure in
The Professor's House, avers that "happiness is something one can't
explain." Is it, though? Through her knack for turning facts into
ideas, Willa Cather in her novels turns our own minds on in ways
only masterly novelists can do.

Serious novels and stories stir thought by dramatizing, by setting out (usually) moral conflict undergone by believable characters, by replacing argument with human illustration. Where but in
a story, "The Kreutzer Sonata," would one come across the thought
that it is a great delusion "that beauty is goodness." In Tolstoy,
again, death, in his "The Death of Ivan Ilych," is made real in a way
no theologian has ever been able make it. Dickens's Mr. Micawber
brings home the lesson of economy better than any professional
economist has ever done, when in *David Copperfield* he announces:
"Annual income twenty pounds, annual expenditure nineteen
[pounds] nineteen [shillings] and six [pence], result happiness.
Annual income twenty pounds, annual expenditure twenty pounds
ought and six, result misery."

All this and more is why one can reread the great novelists,
always learning new things from them at different stages of one's
own life.¶

XV.

IS THERE A SO-CALLED CANON, or elite grouping or body, of the great novels on which most people would agree? Literary critics set canons; university professors reinforce them. Every even moderately sophisticated reader will have his own personal canon.

The English critic F. R. Leavis, in his book *The Great Tradition* (1948), restricted the great English novelists to four: Jane Austen, George Eliot, Henry James, and Joseph Conrad. He allowed Charles Dickens was a genius, but held his genius was more in the line of entertainer. Leavis later placed D. H. Lawrence in his great tradition, the Lawrence who wrote that "the novel can help us to live as nothing else can." Leavis's own writing tended to the rebarbative, his style being chiefly polemical, and many other critics and readers thought him too restrictive in his selection of the great novelists; other felt that he had vastly overpraised D. H. Lawrence. One recalls that Bertrand Russell once said of D. H. Lawrence that "he is a writer of a certain descriptive power whose ideas cannot be too soon forgot."

In the United States, the critic Harold Bloom, more catholic in his taste than Leavis, included among his canonical novelists Jane Austen, Stendhal, Balzac, Dickens, the Brontës, Dostoyevsky, Thomas Hardy, Melville, James Joyce, Virginia Woolf, and William Faulkner. "Faulkner's legacy is extensive," he wrote, "and includes such varied figures as Robert Penn Warren, Ralph Ellison, Flannery O'Connor, Gabriel Márquez, and Cormac McCarthy." He cites the latter's *Blood Meridian*, along with Philip Roth's *Sabbath's Theater*, Don DeLillo's *Underworld*, and Thomas Pynchon's *Mason & Dixon* "as the four grand narratives composed by living Americans." Bloom digresses slightly to remark that for him there "are several candidates for the great American book, and none of them is exactly a novel: *The Scarlet Letter, Moby-Dick, Leaves of Grass*, Emerson's *Essays*, and *Huckleberry Finn.*" Why *The Scarlet Letter, Moby-Dick*, and *Huckleberry Finn* are not exactly novels he doesn't say. He is also high on Toni Morrison. Bloom believes what he calls "the Protestant Will" the "single thematic vision that links together the traditions of the Anglo-American novel," and ends by writing that "it may be that the Protestant Will and the novel are now dying together, and that something beyond the revival of an eccentric romance form is yet to come."

For Lionel Trilling, the four transcendently great novelists were Cervantes, Dickens, Dostoyevsky, and Proust. For Irving Howe they included Stendhal, Dostoyevsky, André Malraux, Arthur Koestler, and the George Orwell of *Nineteen Eighty-Four*. Edmund Wilson, excellent critic though he was, perhaps owing to his atheist's strict rationalist temperament, was unable to appreciate Kafka or Conrad; and because of this same atheism, Wilson felt that Evelyn Waugh's best novel, *Brideshead Revisited*, was not only ruined by its religious theme but marked by something akin to a sell-out on the part of its author.

That some novels have won official prizes is no help in determining which are the important, let alone the great novels. The Pulitzer Prize for Fiction has long been disqualified by having been given to second- and third-rate novels. One gathers that the Booker Prize in England is not much better. As for the Nobel Prize for Literature, a finer club could be made of those writers who while still alive didn't win it—Tolstoy, Proust, Henry James,

Virginia Woolf, Vladimir Nabokov, *et alia*—than those who did: Pearl Buck, Hermann Hesse, Sinclair Lewis, John Steinbeck, *et alia*. Rare is the critic who can fairly estimate what is not to his taste. I do not myself pretend to be that critic. Like the good philistine in the art museum, I know what I like: my own canon would include all the great Russian novelists and short-story writers, from Nikolai Gogol to Vasily Grossman and Aleksander Solzhenitsyn; the Victorians Dickens, Eliot, Trollope; the Americans Cooper, Hawthorne, Melville, James, Wharton, Cather. If there is any heterodoxy in my canon it lies perhaps in my thinking Willa Cather the best American novelist of the past century. In *O, Pioneers!* and *My Ántonia*, and many of her stories, she took on the great American subject of immigration; in *Death Comes for the Archbishop* and *Shadows on the Rock* and *The Professor's House*, she wrote about the power of tradition inherent in religion; in *The Song of the Lark* she provided the best novel we have of the interior life of the artist. And she did all these things with consummate literary skill, a calm philosophical detachment, and an unwavering confidence in the truth of the imagination.

I recently made a list of the lesser known novels and novelists who over the years have given me pleasure and, I like to think, broadened my outlook and deepened my culture, while, I like to tell myself, may have made me a touch smarter about both the world and myself. Here, in no special order, is a list of twenty-six novelists and short-story writers and a few of their works who have performed such a service for me, all of whom, given world enough and time, I can easily imagine re-reading.

- Paul Scott (*The Raj Quartet*)
- Tomasi di Lampedusa (*The Leopard*)
- William Faulkner (*The Snopes Trilogy*, a few excellent stories)
- Joseph Roth (*The Radetzky March*)

- Edith Wharton *(The Age of Innocence, The House of Mirth)*
- Muriel Spark *(Memento Mori, The Prime of Miss Jean Brodie)*
- Dan Jacobson *(Time of Arrival, The Zulu and the Zeide)*
- Max Beerbohm *(Zuleika Dobson, Seven Men)*
- V. S. Naipaul *(A House for Mr Biswas, Guerrillas)*
- Varlam Shalamov *(Kolyma Stories)*
- Evelyn Waugh *(Brideshead Revisited)*
- Sholem Aleichem *(Tevye the Dairyman* and the *Railroad Stories)*
- Marguerite Yourcenar *(Memoirs of Hadrian)*
- Anthony Powell *(A Dance to the Music of Time)*
- E. M. Forster *(Howards End)*
- Penelope Fitzgerald *(The Bookshop, The Blue Flower)*
- I. J. Singer *(The Brothers Ashkenazi, The Family Carnovsky)*
- Elizabeth Bowen *(The Death of the Heart)*
- Chaim Grade *(The Yeshiva, The Agunah)*
- Richard Wright *(Native Son)*
- Mary Gaitskill *(Bad Behavior, Don't Cry)*
- Ivan Goncharov *(Oblomov, A Common Story)*
- Heinrich Heine *(The Harz Journey, The Rabbi of Bacharach)*
- Richard Russo *(Empire Falls)*
- Milton Steinberg *(As a Driven Leaf)*
- R. K. Narayan *(The Guide)*

And here are six novelists and short-story writers whom I feel I do not need to read again:

- Graham Greene, whose combination of leftwing politics and Catholicism has never worked for me.
- Alice Munro, whose stories of infidelity in provincial Canada have always seemed to me of limited interest.
- George Orwell, whose great work was in the essay, and whose novels, apart from the famous and politically useful *Nineteen Eighty-Four*, fail to come alive.

- Toni Morrison, with whose novels I have never had any luck, and have concluded are more for teaching than reading.
- Jonathan Franzen, who seems in his fiction to write about people to whom he can feel superior.
- S. Y. Agnon, four of whose novels I've read, always with high expectation, never with satisfaction, though I am told he is a writer who must be read in the Hebrew in which he wrote.

Then there are those younger novelists and short-story writers I read but do not have settled views about: Allegra Goodman, Joshua Cohen, Michael Chabon, Jonathan Safran Foer, Colson Whitehead, and a few others.❡

XVI.

WHAT WOULD A WORLD without fiction be like? Many—most—people perhaps wouldn't notice any difference. But for that minority interested in the oddity of human character, in the role that fortune and fate play in human destiny, in the vast variousness and richness of human possibility, in the contradictoriness of human nature, the absence of fiction would be a major subtraction and a towering sadness.

If all writers were left to write about were strictly factual matters, how impoverished the world would not merely seem but be! Writers would be restricted to memoir, articles, essays, mere factual material. So much that is best suited to novels and stories would be lost. As an example, there was for many years a Chicago bookseller named Stuart Brent, who ran a successful bookshop on the city's posh Michigan Avenue. A genuine character, Stuart was passionate in his opinions and entirely unaware of repression in conversation. "How go things, Stuart?" I might greet him upon entering his shop. "How could they be going?" he replied, in his usual stentorian voice. "The *goyim* are killing me." (By the *goyim*, I suspect he meant Walden Books and other mail-order book sellers of the day.) Stuart stocked books for many of the psychiatrists and psychoanalysts who had offices along Michigan Avenue and had no difficulty mocking them to their faces. I watched him once push one of my own books on a young psychoanalyst, saying, "Read this. You might learn something." The sales manager at W. W. Norton, then my publisher, told me that he once called Stuart about a bill he owed that was ninety days overdue. "I'll put the check in the mail today," Stuart said. "But while I have you on the phone, do know that it would help a lot if you didn't publish such shitty books." He was also capable of acts of great generosity, and saw his third, much-younger-than-he wife through a long bout of dementia. He had ten children with three wives. He was, Stuart, a true character.

I suppose by questioning his children and learning more about him, I could have written a memoir about Stuart Brent after his death. Instead I chose to put a Stuart-like character into a short story which I published under the title "The Bernie Klepner Show." In my story I exchanged Stuart's bookshop for a radio talk show in which the main character expressed himself without qualification or tact. The story is narrated by one of the sons.

A sports fan as a kid, I stayed up one night to hear him [my father] interview Kareem Abdul Jabbar, recently retired from the Los Angeles Lakers. "Mr. Jabbar," my father said, "what does it say about our country that a man like you can become famous and a multi-millionaire because he is inordinately tall and has acquired the knack of throwing a rubber ball through a metal hoop?" . . . On the air my father once asked Mayor Daley—the son not the father—if corruption was absolutely necessary to run a big city, or, as in the case of Chicago, was the rampant corruption instead only an Irish thing? I heard him begin an interview with Bill Clinton, then promoting his memoir, if he had any interests in life apart from sex, money, and power. He had the editor of *Poetry Magazine* on and asked him how he felt about his job now that poetry had become a mere intramural sport, read only by the people who were writing it. He asked Jesse Jackson how he had the gall to mount his own pulpit after it was revealed he had a child out of wedlock. Why people put themselves through my father's buzz-saw by appearing on his show I never understood, but they did, five nights a week, for decades.

Another example comes from the life of a less than close friend, who shall here remain nameless, who in his career went from success to success without any explanation of why, working at higher and higher jobs at magazines, the State Department, at newspapers, in publishing, in universities, at foundations. He had wealthy and connected parents, true, and made further connections of his own when a student at Harvard. He was possessed of inoffensive, somewhat aristocratic good looks; he talked the talk and talked it well. But at none of the institutions at which he worked did he depart leaving the slightest mark. How did this happen? How did he bring it off? Did his outward success bring him any inward happiness? Only fiction, it seemed to me, could hope to consider, I do not say solve, the puzzle that was his career and attempt to answer the questions it left in its wake, and so I wrote a story about it called "Just the Man for the Job."¶

XVII.

I HAVE NEVER THOUGHT of myself as a critic, but instead as an ardent reader who has been lucky enough to turn a few dollars by writing about some of the things he has read. For three years or so during the 1980s, I was asked to do this on a regular basis for *Commentary Magazine*, writing about what seemed to be not the best-selling but the most ambitious new fiction of the day. Along with *Partisan Review* and *Encounter*, *Commentary* was devoted to the highbrow standard of art. In these magazines such critics as Mary McCarthy and Dwight Macdonald disqualified J. D. Salinger, Tennessee Williams, Arthur Miller, and others as not up to the standard. The critic, in this intellectual environment, was a gate-keeper of high art, working to make sure that no one unqualified was allowed into the holy pantheon.

During my days writing about new fiction for *Commentary* not many got past during my shift at the gate. I wrote what were essentially put-downs of the fiction of Robert Stone, John Irving, Joan Didion, Renata Adler, Ann Beattie, S. J. Perelman, Cynthia Ozick, Gabriel García Márquez, John Updike, Philip Roth, and others. In writing about Bernard Malamud, whose book of stories, *The Magic Barrel* I much admired and whose novel *The Fixer* I continue to think a genuinely great book, I found myself commenting on the sad slide downward of his last novels. This may seem hard, and in some ways it is, but as I look over this list of novelists whose books once caused a stir, I find that I was more right than not in thinking that interest in their fiction wouldn't last—as indeed it hasn't.

Many among these writers had highbrow ambition (Cynthia Ozick), dazzling literary gifts (Gabriel García Márquez), a taste for big subjects (Robert Stone), a willingness to experiment (Renata Adler), but somehow it wasn't enough—enough to cause their writing to be readable now, thirty-five or so years later. What was missing?

I have throughout these pages referred to "serious" novels and stories. Time—perhaps past time—that I explain what I mean by "serious." By "serious" I mean novels and stories that possess a certain unmistakable gravity—fiction that implicitly asks the right questions, even if it doesn't supply complete or satisfactory answers to them. They take human nature as the great puzzle it is and set out to connect a few of its vast number of pieces. Through the technique they learned as masters of fiction, they put the breath of life into their characters, and through these characters they explore the conundrums life poses for us all. Avoiding the abstraction of philosophy, they are themselves philosophical, and philosophical about the matters that mean most to all of us: family, love, ambition, and so much more. Serious novels investigate ideas, frequently find them wanting, sometimes helping to kill them. In the latter category think of Arthur Koestler's *Darkness at Noon*, George Orwell's *Nineteen Eighty-Four*, Aleksandr Solzhenitsyn's *One Day in the Life of Ivan Denisovich*. These three novels did more damage to the prestige of Communism than any straightforward polemic or personal account of the hell of living under that cruel system of government. I like to think that fictional accounts, in a quieter way, put a dent or two into the less-evil but still dopey ideas of "the open marriage," "the mid-life crisis," and other foolish passing fancies. I await the novel that will put paid to the therapeutic culture generally.❡

XVIII.

LIKE INSTITUTIONS AND PEOPLE, artistic forms and genres lose their prestige. Fair to say that contemporary visual art does not hold the cultural interest it did fifty or so years ago. Atonal music, once the music of choice of the avant-garde, has never lived up to its promise. Much the same can be said about contemporary poetry. Not since the death of Philip Larkin in 1985 has there been a poet who has commanded the attention of people who think of themselves as literary in their instincts and interests. In all these realms—visual art, music, poetry—we can of course live off the culture of the past, which, praise be, is enough to sustain us, yet that its continuation into our day and beyond is in doubt is, more than troubling, a genuine subtraction from the richness of life. And now one begins to wonder if the novel, the supreme literary genre, that paramount purveyor of education and entertainment over the past two centuries, is also in its contemporary form losing its hold on readers, literary artists, the culture generally?

What, really, do we lose if the novel no longer has an important place in our culture? To put the question the other way round, what really have we gained by reading about people who never really existed living through events that didn't actually happen? The argument of this book has been that without the help of the novel we lose the hope of gaining a wider and, in the instances of the great novelists, more complex view of life, its mystery, its meaning, its point. If we lose this, we are forced to fall back on the rather sterile concepts and ideas that current-day philosophy and social science along with pop psychology and high-flown journalism provide. The novel at its best demonstrates the thinness of most such intellectual constructs, and seeks to discover deeper truths, the truth of the imagination, the truth of human nature, the truth of the heart. To turn to the question put by this book's title, *The Novel, Who Needs It?*, the answer is that we all do, including even people who wouldn't think of reading novels—we all need it, and in this, the great age of distraction we may just need it more than ever before.❡

ACKNOWLEDGMENTS

~

*I wish to thank Edward Blum
for encouraging me to write this book
and the Gale Foundation for its financial support.*

BIBLIOGRAPHY

≈

Bakhtin, Mikhail. "Discourse in the Novel." In *The Dialogic Imagination: Four Essays by Mikhail Bakhtin,* edited by Michael Holquist, translated by Caryl Emerson and Michael Holquist. Austin: University of Texas Press, 1981.

Bloom, Harold. *Novelists and Novels: A Collection of Critical Essays.* New York: Checkmark Books, 2007.

Bottum, Joseph. *The Decline of the Novel.* South Bend: St. Augustine's Press, 2019.

Cecil, David. *Early Victorian Novelists.* New York: Penguin Books, 1948.

Cecil, David. *The Fine Art of Reading.* London: Souvenir Press Ltd, 2001.

De Goncourt, Edmond and Jules. *Pages from the Goncourt Journals.* Translated by Robert Baldick. New York: New York Review of Books Classics, 2006.

Ford, Ford Madox. *The English Novel: From the Earliest Days to the Death of Joseph Conrad.* Manchester: Carcanet Press, 1983.

Forster, E. M. *Aspects of the Novel.* Boston: Mariner Books, 1956.

Frye, Northrop. *Anatomy of Criticism.* Princeton: Princeton University Press, 2000.

Grossman, Vasily. *Life and Fate*. Translated by Robert Chandler. New York: New York Review of Books Classics, 2006.

Howe, Irving. *Politics and the Novel*. Chicago: Ivan R. Dee, 2002.

Kenner, Hugh. *Historical Fictions*. Athens: University of Georgia Press, 1995.

Kundera, Milan. *The Art of the Novel*. New York: Harper Perennial Modern Classics, 2003.

Lawrence, D. H. *The Bad Side of Books, Selected Essays*. New York: NYRB Classics, 2019.

Leavis, F. R. *The Great Tradition*. New York: Penguin Books Ltd, 1972.

Leavis, Q. D. *Fiction and the Reading Public*. Dorset: Pimlico, 2000.

Lubbock, Percy. *The Craft of Fiction*. Amsterdam: Leopold Classic Library, 2015.

Lukacs, Georg. *The Theory of the Novel*. Translated by Anna Bostock. Cambridge: The MIT Press, 1974.

Macdonald, Dwight. *Against the American Grain*. New York: Random House, 1962.

Najder, Zdzisław. *Joseph Conrad: A Life*. Rochester: Camden House, 2007.

Rahv, Philip. *Literature and the Sixth Sense*. Boston: Houghton Mifflin, 1970.

Rieff, Philip. *The Triumph of the Therapeutic: Uses of Faith after Freud*. Wilmington: Intercollegiate Studies Institute, 2006.

Roth, Henry. *Call It Sleep: A Novel*. New York: Picador, 2005.

Saintsbury, George. *The English Novel*. Glasgow: Good Press, 2019.

Tolstoy, Leo. *Great Short Works of Leo Tolstoy*. Translated by Louise Maude, Aylmer Maude, J. D. Duff, Sam A. Carmack, and John Bayley. New York: Perennial Classics, 2004.

Trilling, Lionel. *The Liberal Imagination.* New York: New York Review Books Classics, 2008.

Turgenev, Ivan. *Fathers and Sons.* Translated by Richard Freeborn. New York: Oxford University Press, 2008.

Watt, Ian. *The Rise of the Novel: Studies in Defoe, Richardson and Fielding.* Oakland: University of California Press, 2001.

Wolf, Maryanne. *Proust and the Squid: The Story and Science of the Reading Brain.* New York: Harper Perennial, 2008.

INDEX

~